I0518515

NEVER SAID A WORD

A Memoir of Survival

The Cost of Silence and The Power of Truth

By

Fonda E. Woodard

This work reflects actual events in the life of the author as truthfully as recollection permits. Some events have been compressed, and some dialogue has been recreated.

Copyright 2025 by Fonda E. Woodard

Cover design By: Salaam Muhammad

For more information, address:
info.neversaidaword@gmail.com

Ebook ISBN: 979-8-9991669-1-3
Paperback ISBN: 979-8-9991669-2-0
Hardcover ISBN: 979-8-9991669-0-6

DEDICATION

To those who have been abandoned, silenced and harmed by sexual trauma.

To those who live quietly, carrying the weight of what was done to them.

May you find the strength to speak truth to power and the healing you so deeply deserve.

To my husband, Charles, thank you for your unconditional love, unwavering support, and for loving me exactly as I am.

To my family, your encouragement has given me the courage to speak, to write, and to stand.

This is for all of us.

TABLE OF CONTENTS

PREFACE

Before you read these words, please heed this warning: This book is for every little girl who has ever considered suicide. If this is not you, there may be many more of us than you would like to know. I've written this work to let you know there is hope in stopping the silent cycle of inconceivable pain by acknowledging everyday atrocities to humanity and speaking truth to power through disclosure and revelations about the wrongs of our past.

My story is one of resilience. It's about a young Black girl coming of age in post-civil rights era Virginia, where the James River meets the Chesapeake Bay. Depending on the day, life could be sweet or sour in the southeastern city of Newport News. Riding on my granddaddy's boat in the summertime with the breeze and sunlight simultaneously kissing my skin, I couldn't help but feel fully alive. On land, where my friends and I would gather handfuls of flowers for the dandelion wine our fathers loved to prepare, I was just as secure in my joy. The days of my youth skipped by as if perfectly set for me to live out loud, completely safe and carefree. That was until I learned how easily senseless acts could silence a voice like mine and how effective that silence could be at stirring the fears of an adult far removed from the past.

When I was a child, I spent a lot of time discovering myself through the eyes of others. After facing colorism, sexual abuse, abandonment, and the responsibility of holding in family secrets that nearly tore me apart, piece by piece, much of my experience left me scarred with shame and insecurities that took a while to grow out of. The heart of this book focuses on what I endured during that time and my breakthrough journey to heal. When terrible things happened to me, I never said a word about them. On the surface, I was afraid of retaliation. Deep down, I was embarrassed by what had happened to me. Reliving the past, I was the victim, yet I was ashamed of what I had done to survive. Shame's favorite meal is secrecy. No one should ever feel that their words do not hold weight in their well-being, yet those were my exact emotions for too long. I hope that this work will help you feel different. I pray that by reading about what I've gone through and what I've been able to overcome, you're encouraged to raise your voice, speak truth to power, and experience liberation. I am blessed to discover this after years of using silence as my best answer to unthinkable trauma.

Though I was born in 1964 and left Newport News in 1983, it wasn't until the COVID-19 pandemic that I began to find and use every part of my voice. The parts of my voice I thought were long gone, shattered and scattered by years of abuse, leaving them without sound or a coherent story to tell, had risen back up. Most days, I wanted to use those parts to scream at the top of my lungs as I'd never done before, to make all the pain from the past and present finally go away. Between witnessing the intense political climate, emerging evidence of ongoing racial injustices with the murder of George Floyd in Minnesota, and the Black Lives Matter enduring fight for equality for people of color, simply managing everyday burdens took on a greater dimension of survival. You could turn on the news, listen to any radio station, or spend a few minutes scrolling through social media, and there it was on wide display: our sacred Black lives intertwined with a new age of overt public lynching. And much of this display seemed up for debate as if it were 'fake news' or a long-held delusion by those who are oppressed. In short, pandemic life was exhausting—emotionally and physically taxing to the point of insanity.

Like many caught amid changing times, I grew restless, tired of trying to contain the lid on top of a bubbling pot of fear, anxiety, and my fight-or-flight instincts. It is a strange thing to feel both angry and helpless. On more days than I can count, I simply wanted to say "Fuck the flight," and start whooping ass and fight. Although I've always known better than to pick fights, I ain't never been one to back down from one either. I had grown weary of the concept of being the bigger person. As a grown adult, trying my best to remain calm and cordial made sense. But I can admit the little girl in me had not yet accepted the prestigious words of Michelle Obama, "When they go low, we go high." The broken voice of my childhood self longed to scream out, preferably in the face of anyone who'd hurt us from the time of our birth up until the moment in 2020 when I recognized how difficult coping with it all had become.

Contagion confinement affects communities differently. In the Black community, the Blackdemic was an imperfect storm that stretched our attention spans razor-thin. Protest after protest unfolded over the same egregious issues we'd been up against since Dr. Martin Luther King Jr. shared his dream of equality with the world. Our external conflicts, mixed with internal traumas, quickly foamed to the surface as if they'd been called forth by the times to haunt us from the past. In my daily life, seclusion became an uninvited old and familiar friend.

Prayer, meditation, and binge-watching Netflix provided a brief respite from a vicious 24-hour news cycle. Documentaries, having always been my programming preference, gave me a chance to escape the depression that followed my isolation. Sitting alone in my room at home in front of the television, wrapped up in blankets and snacks close at hand, I found comfort in the retelling of stories by strangers whose testimonials were likely to resonate with me on a cellular level.

The documentaries I love the most are those that reveal the heroism of the underdog. That is who I've always rooted for. I feel simpatico with the underdog because it's the story of my life. Not only can I relate deeply to the feeling of being overlooked and underestimated, but I've also grown to respect those stories that have a way of broadening perspectives and challenging ideas of the big-picture view. Revelations such as these are immensely valuable. When we think of underdogs, it forces us to face the full scope of a deeper meaning of the story told and the individual implications of our connections.

Every voice counts, and each has a story to tell. When an underdog's story gets told, listeners have no choice but to reexamine the saying, *'What you don't know won't hurt you."* Oh, but it does! The stories that give voice to the voiceless often shed light on the truth, inspiring us to rise above our greatest obstacles. The key to remember is that setbacks are not the end of the road but rather a detour from the planned route. By highlighting the importance of resilience in the face of adversity, they offer us hope and optimism as we ponder if that positive change is possible. Such narratives teach us that the human spirit is capable of incredible feats, allowing us to realize that no upset is too great to overcome with the right mindset and suitable support. Without telling underdog stories, we wouldn't be encouraged to think critically about justice, fairness, and rigid power dynamics that seldom favor the little guy. Without the information that affirms we're not alone in an isolating experience, many of us would be hard-pressed to find the strength to stand up for who we are and what we believe in. The stories of underdogs breathe new life into the untenable strength that lies within us all. Come hell or high water, if we know it's possible to win, our spirits won't be afraid to challenge the status quo. These are some reasons I've chosen to share my story today after holding it in for 50-some-odd years.

During one of my many binge-sessions during the nationwide lockdown, I decided to put on the documentary "Surviving R. Kelly." Before I thought about starting the first episode, Netflix had advertised for a while, maybe a few months. There was a time when R. Kelly could do no wrong. When you're a famous R&B artist who puts out hit after hit for decades on end, people aren't as critical of the misgivings in your private life. Somewhere along the way, that cloak of invisibility ran out. By 2019, Kelly had spent at least half of his career defending his image in the court of public opinion, within the city limits of New York and Chicago, and among countless litigators. Despite the buzz surrounding the survivors' coalition sounding off in a three-part series that had appeared on the Lifetime network, a station branded as 'television for women,' I knew this particular documentary wouldn't be as enjoyable as something less painfully close to home. Based on all the reviews I'd heard and previews I'd come across, I didn't have to guess that the series would trigger me emotionally. But when my thumb pressed hard on the remote control to select 'Play,' I was ready. I had to watch it. I only prayed that all the therapy and self-care I'd done up to that point would not be lost while I let the images unfold across the screen.

Detailing the sexual abuse allegations that would later lead to Kelly's arrest and a 30-year prison sentence, a slew of young Black women found the courage to open wounds that years of scar tissue had aided in quieting. For so long, several parties worked tirelessly to bury their words. In some cases, the women could count themselves in that number. But with the support of each other's stories, they each began sharing details that made it hard to deny any wrongdoing. As they recounted some of their most profound, darkest experiences with their abuser, each woman spun a tale of unlawful conditioning and stomach-turning sex crimes. Children, yet barely teenagers when the abuse began, they'd been groomed to believe that what they were experiencing was not worthy of the loudest alarm. Hearing more about what they endured took me back to the dark places of my own life.

The tales of pain mixed with shame and confusion went on and on as each episode rolled into the next. My body stayed still and stuck in one place; my jawbones clinched, and my muscles tensed from the focused attention I held on every story recounting hurtful moments that felt overwhelmingly familiar. Their testimonials stirred my soul with memories from my youth, making me realize those young women weren't strangers. They were me, and I was them, as tears rolled.

I had only told a few girlfriends before then who knew the depth of my pain. You see, I knew what it was like to be taken advantage of by powerful predators. I remembered the molestation, the grooming, and the feeling of being like prey left to fend for myself in the lions' den, a precious lamb set for the slaughter.

Before I knew it, my eyes were full of tears. I felt a connection with those women that made me feel their pain through the remembrance of mine. However, it was their courage that moved me the most. Their message told me I wasn't alone in the world. I hadn't been the only one to endure sexual abuse, but with me being at least 20 years older than most of the women who appeared, it was sadly apparent that I had not been the last. This was a wake-up call. But it wasn't until after encountering a tweet displaying the hashtag '#METOO' that I finally found the confidence to answer that call to action and share a few lost words of my own.

CHAPTER 1

Colored Outside The Lines

Unlike the rest of my kinfolk, my skin was dark, and my hair was coarse. Not only was I the "black sheep" of the family, but I also had the nerve to be tender-headed. Unfortunately, my grandparents never believed in burning hair to straighten it with a hot comb. So, instead of working with a clean slate of flattened curls, my grandmother would lock my skinny little body between her knees and drag the comb through my hair with the strength of a mule. My hair tangled so severely that I would cry until I felt a POP right where her hands had been feverishly working. It was my grandmother doing her best to restrain me. Her weapon of choice was a comb the length of a school ruler with teeth like a piranha. Some may know it as that rat tail comb–a staple in every Black woman's beauty drawer. Now, every time I see one of those combs, I can feel the pain of the breaking of hair and pops of beads in what Black folk call your "kitchen."

During those hours of tortured grooming, while feeling like my scalp was being separated from my skull, I would glance at the porcelain skin on my grandmother's legs and remember how I was the complete opposite of everyone surrounding me. All my immediate family members were light-skinned with straight hair. Sometimes, it was a little wavy, but their hair was always fine and flowing. Mine was thick and nappy. That's how others had described it. So, that's how I described myself. As a double whammy to my grandmother, whose task was to take care of it, my hair was as long as it was unruly.

My skin was dark enough to make me ashamed whenever somebody pulled out a paper bag. Remember the times we were in?

Where I grew up, in Newport News, Virginia, in the '60s and '70s, Black folks were the most color-struck kind of folks, including my family, keeping it honest. The U.S. Supreme Court landmark case Brown vs. Board of Education decided that state-sponsored segregation in public schools was unconstitutional. However, the city's road to integration was painfully slow due to then-Senator Harry Byrd's "massive resistance" against the decision. Integration wasn't realized until 17 years later, in August 1971, the year I turned seven and entered first grade at Carver Elementary.

Sometimes, it was as if we were even more segregated within our Black communities, at times, than from the whites'. My lived experience was adhering to the standards set by that brown paper bag daily in my household. I was exposed to one central thing that stood out in my mind, it was that light-skinned people seemed like they were the dominant species of the Black race. I was thinking like this as a child. Imagine that.

For me, suddenly, somehow, you were better if you were lighter. If there were a dispute about beauty, fair skin over brown skin, fair skin would always win. If there was ever an argument over who was right or wrong, the assumption most often held was that the fair-skinned person knew more or better. Superiority was about your shade to whiteness, and thus, in warped minds, if you were a light-skinned Black person, you were superior. My granddaddy would often say, *"White folk think 'cause they white–they right."* And I thought when Black folks are light, they believe they 'more right' than dark skin folk. It was sad. But I know I wasn't the only one with this opinion or experience growing up in Southeastern Virginia during that era. It was just the way some people thought and were taught to think.

The notion of passing, being able to move seamlessly within and between two separate worlds, undoubtedly brought a feeling of superiority that I would never experience. I was dark brown. And I would fail the paper bag test every time. To add insult to injury, I had a severe case of eczema in my childhood that would flare up if I got scared or nervous about anything. It was dyshidrotic eczema, where stress is the trigger. I'd break out in a scaly rash and small blisters across a stretch of skin that included my neck, the pits of my elbows, the upper back of my calves, my hairline, and, oh good Lord–my dominant hand was the worst. Some days, I could hardly hold a pencil or write a sentence using my right hand. I was just one big mess. The scarring of my eczema would end up leaving my skin darker than it was before and leather-like in texture, leaving me self-conscious about my body. Whether I was happily playing all day in the hot Virginia sun or facing some of my worst moments of anxiety and shame, I'd walk away feeling like a little black ugly duckling. In those days, the negative feelings about my looks began to take root deep in my soul.

I still believe that nobody in my family dealt with more issues over their appearance than I did. Light-skinned people have an easier time, in my young mind. From what I experienced, they seemed more socially acceptable than darker people. Moreover, it was like light-skinned Black folk were less intimidated by white folks than dark-skinned Black folks. The seemingly more effortless life continued from skin to hair. My family members had the kind of hair that most people called "good hair" for being easier to wash, comb, and style. Of course, as a child, you think as such. So, I chalk it up to my childlike innocence or ignorance, but I thought the only "bad hair" was no hair. Regardless, I was still insecure about my looks. It was through the silent cues of others that those insecurities often materialized. My grandparents, mother, aunt, and uncle seemed to move through life with a better advantage. None of them ever gave me the impression that they dealt with colorism the way others may have because of their appearance.

My grandparents hailed from the Tribal Nation of Haliwa-Saponi Indians. The Haliwa-Saponi are Native American Peoples of the North East Piedmont region of the State of North Carolina. The name Haliwa is derived from the two counties of Halifax and

Warren, the ancestral homelands of the Saponi People dating back to the early 18th century.

My grandparents' homeland was recognized in 1965 as a tribe by the North Carolina legislature, claiming the state's coastal tribes and the Accomac, Cherokee, Nansemond, Occaneechi, Saponi, Tuscarora, and Tutelo Indians as ancestors. However, nearly 400 Haliwa tribal members successfully brought suit in Halifax County court to correct the racial designation on their birth certificates, marriage, and driver's licenses to "Indian." Before the "correction," they were considered Black. By the 1800s, when European settlers had colonized the United States for almost a century, Indian people were living more Westernized lives than ever before, to the point that the distinction between Indian and non-Indian was obscured. As their isolated communities had been pushed to the fringes of the country, they became just invisible enough to offer refuge or permanent homes to runaway slaves, as well as free Blacks, white criminals, and other whites who were dissatisfied with mainstream society. Episodic matings and marriages within these communities led to a mix of features that led white lawmakers to consider most Indians to be white/Black mixtures, using terms such as "yellow people" in the North Carolina Piedmont area or "Cane River mulattos," in the New Orleans Region and, to emphasize the idea that people could only be of Black and white descent or a mix of the two. When the members of these groups are mentioned in early official records, such as court documents or census tables, they are frequently referred to as "free persons of color." In many areas, there was a conscious effort on the part of the whites to push the Indian people into the Black category for better economic turnout. For example, there were Black and white schools in parts of Virginia and North Carolina before I attended school. Designating Indians as 'either-or' saved the state the expense of establishing a third school system.

As it was, Indigenous folks who were too dark or ethnic-looking to pass as white became light-skinned Black folks. And though racism didn't quite work in their favor, colorism sure did. This is a common occurrence for Native people across the South, particularly those not living on reservations. The majority of the Native population in southern states have lived for generations as a third race in a society split between Black and white. The brown paper bag test would determine how they should be treated.

Surrounded by the James and York Rivers and the Chesapeake Bay, Newport News was filled with hard-working people. Our city's primary employers are the Newport News Shipbuilding and Dry Dock, the military, and their contractors. Between the shipyard and the military bases, they kept people employed from as close as the neighborhood to as far away as the Carolinas. Fort Eustis Army, Langley Air Force, and Naval Bases in Norfolk and Yorktown, most now known as "joint bases," make Newport News a heavy military and civil servant town. My grandfather worked briefly in the shipyard and later as a United States Postal Service postal worker. He was well-respected within our community. The way he worked was louder than his skin color had to do with his success or advantage. I know it didn't matter to him what he looked like because he was a man of integrity.

My granddaddy was a great man. He was always productive. He had a matchless grind and work ethic that I've continued to admire long after his passing. For a man with limited education, he was not limited in how he thought, saved, invested, and helped his family. He and my grandmother never received formal education beyond the third grade, but that never stopped them from ensuring their children needed anything. Like many people during their childhoods, they were forced to quit grade school to help their families make a living, usually in the fields. I can assume that facing the challenges of their lives outside the classroom only served their success in adulthood, at least in some areas.

For the most part, we lived modestly, but I always felt like we were rich. My granddaddy had a truck, a car, a tractor, a boat, a "brick" house, money in the bank, and savings bonds by the hundreds. That was much more than I thought most people in town may have owned. If he weren't tending to those possessions, he would have been tending to the five gardens he kept around our community. To keep some people's lots from overgrowing and looking unkempt, bringing down the property value in the neighborhood, he'd grab his equipment, hop on his tractor, and go from yard to yard, tilling the land. When it came time to harvest, he'd feed the neighbors, letting them have free reign to take whatever they wanted; he just had to know what they were getting. According to him, they were considered stealing if he didn't know who was taking what. His philosophy was that if you steal from one, you steal from all. And what you stole could go to somebody who needs it.

My grandfather used to have a bunch of sayings he'd pass out like candy on Halloween, which is an interesting analogy to place here because my grandparents never let me go out trick or treating. They loved the Lord and were God-fearing but weren't particularly always staying up in church. Still, something about dressing up in monstrous costumes to roam the city in search of sweets struck them as teetering wicked. Even though many other people did it, dressing up was not the question I dared not ask. Eating other people's treats was a no-no as well. The saying, "You can't eat from er'body's kitchen," was threaded in our household commandments. When I was growing up, there had been a string of incidents where people had found broken glass and razor blades in the things strangers had given them on Halloween night. "We'll get you a bunch of candy. If you want candy," he'd add. "But you ain't going out trick or treating."

It's funny how easy it is to remember those sayings today as if I can hear my grandfather's voice saying them now. As I've gotten older, I find myself repeating many of the same things he used to say over and over. One of his sayings was, "There are three things I can't stand: a liar, a thief, and a lying thief." The line that often followed that one was, "Cause' if you will lie, you will steal. If you steal, you will cheat. You gotta earn it. It can be the easy way or the hard way, but you gotta earn it." There were so many more.

Whenever he found me crying about something, he'd say one of two things. "Stop all that crying. You can't see your future through your tears." Or, "Baby, I can't understand a damn thang you are saying. You gone have to come back in here and talk to me when you ain't crying about it. Now, hush, come back when you stop."

If I got tongue-tied and caught up trying to explain something, he'd say, "I can't understand what you're saying. You can't understand what you're thinking. Slow down, and let your mind catch up with yo' mouf."

As I matured, his one-liners, like those conversations about relationships, held more weight and hit differently. Some of them were so heavy it's been hard for me to let them go after all this time. Like later in life, when I'd mentioned men to him, "Know that when it comes to men, baby, it's the rule of six," he'd state firmly when I had mentioned a man wasn't doing something. "If he ain't gone do it within the first six hours, he ain't gone to do it within the first six days. If he ain't gone do it within the first six days, he ain't gone to do it in the first six weeks. He ain't gone do it in the first six weeks, he ain't gone do it in the first six months. And if he ain't gone do it in the first six months, don't expect him to do it within the next six years, if at all! Think about it. Is he cooking for you? Is he cleaning for you? Does he want to take you somewhere? Don't want to take you anywhere? A man will show you who he is with his time." Umph, I failed that lesson a time or two.

Another expression he loved to say was, "You can park on my grass; just don't park on my garden. I eat out of my garden. Grass just feels good to my feet—my garden feels good to my belly; grass don't feed me." Him and his gardens used to get on my damn nerves sometimes. I loved that he was so cared for, enough to share with our community, and that he could love and give and allow them to "come to get what you want from the corner" where we lived. It was inspiring to witness his communal portion. But then that meant we had to pick the stuff in the garden, all five in the community, plus the property he owned on Butler Farm Road in Hampton, about a 10-minute drive away. That was a lot of fresh produce.

I thought, *Why don't we just let these people come and pick what they want? Why do we gotta pick it, and then they come, and all they got to do is pick it out of the buckets?* I would beg him to let the community pick. They call it gleaning now. I wanted everybody to come and glean the gardens so my little body could be spared the hard labor. He'd say, "Nope. Er'body don't know how to pick, ain't going to tear my garden up." And that would be the end of the conversation.

My grandmother was my grandfather's life partner of over 60 years and helped with everything, including tending to our five gardens throughout the community. Together, they owned over 40 acres of land throughout Virginia and North Carolina, having acreage in Warrenton and Gaston Lake, North Carolina, and multiple Newport News and Hampton, Virginia properties. My grandmother was always the one who was a part of every deal to make it happen.

My grandmother was a homemaker—a stay-at-home mom, not by choice but out of necessity. I'm sure she had aspirations far beyond homemaking. She could never pursue anything outside our family home for work because she had to care for me. When she quit working to raise me, she found ways to affect how my granddaddy operated when investing in real estate. We did not know it then, but it was 'diversification.' She was in the middle of all my granddaddy's transactions. I remember her saying, "....Odell, you gotta mix thangs up. You need big properties and little properties. You need some properties 'wit' somethin' on it and some wit' nuthin' but trees." Something my grandmother always had: money in her 'breast pocket' —"these the only two suckahs I could trust," she'd say—and an opinion. My grandfather was one of the people I knew of to own stocks, like actual paper stock certificates. That's how they did it back in the day. For my 18th birthday, they gave me stock in what then was Virginia Electric and Power Company (VEPCO). Without my grandmother's influence, I probably wouldn't have gotten those shares to start my own portfolio.

My grandmother is the reason I have such beautiful handwriting. Whether print or cursive—which people don't even know anything about these days—every stroke I put on the page is neat and clean. "The way it looks on paper matters," she'd say. That is because of my grandmother. She was herself all things unruly yet beautiful, after all. When I was growing up, she made it her job to make me practice my writing every day. She also taught me how to tie my tennis shoes. There's no time that I grab my laces now that I don't think about her. She said I was old enough to tie my shoes at age four. She sat me in the middle of the bed and told me, "Don't get off the bed until you know how to tie your tennis shoes." When I got it right, I was so excited I jumped right off.

I don't know if I was more happy to please her or escape a possible whooping. Both my grandparents would whoop me if I got in trouble or disobeyed, but my grandmother could switch you down. Whereas my grandfather would give a simple pop on the arm or a few swats on the behind, she'd take a skinny tree branch from out the yard and go to town on my entire body. She was feisty. Her favorite word was 'shid.' "I ain't putting up with that shid." "I don't know that shid." "Don't nobody know that shid." Or my favorite, "What is that shid?"

Neither one of my grandparents could read well, so I helped out where I could as soon as I learned when I could. What often makes me pause about both is that they weren't wholly illiterate but not confident readers. As I was growing up, still immature and not knowing any better, I never took more time to teach them how to read better. I don't have many regrets because I believe that God ordains all things, but not spending more time teaching them better literacy is one thing. I sometimes wonder how many leaps and bounds we could have made in our achievements if life had not been 'life'n' as hard as it was.

Filling out the medical emergency data cards and the back-to-school papers on the first day of school was always particularly painful. I remember being nervous, confused, and ashamed as they'd lay each item on my desk. It was my responsibility to fill out the cards in class, then take the papers home to my grandparents to read to them, interpret, and have them signed, all while not truly understanding what was written down myself. I was already bewildered before I even got to the point of sharing with them. For more minutes than what seemed appropriate, I'd sit staring at the cards, trying to figure out what to put down for my parental information. I dared not ask for help with what seemed like a simple question.

Even though the beginning of the school year got better as I got older, it was always challenging because it became more routine. I suffered from great agitation and depression from the sheer process of it all. I just wanted to be like the other kids–or so I thought–who put their "real momma and real daddy's name" down on the papers. The truth is I only realized that "my mother" was my grandmother and "daddy" was my granddaddy about two years before I started school, at age five. I knew nothing of the woman who birthed me and the man who kicked rocks and ran because neither of them was present in my infant or developmental years. This confusion was caused by an initial institutionalized family pattern that affected my family dynamics and my relationships and perhaps is what led to long-term emotional and relational consequences. Back in class, I knew if I raised my hand for help, I would have to explain my thinking. Well, it says here to put down the names of my mother and father, but my mother is my grandmother, and my father is my grandfather, so I put their names, right? But I was terrified of being exposed. House rules said, "You 'bet' not tell family bit-ness!" I best keep my mouth shut because "no one needs to know what's happening in our house." I often asked for a hall pass to use the girl's bathroom, where I would sit in a stall and cry it out for a few minutes until I felt I had been away too long. I remember experiencing an overwhelming sadness that would wash over me like a bad mid-summer thunderstorm rolling from the James River. The emotional turbulence was dark and gloomy. It left me feeling sad and alone. That triggered another full-scale of anxiety and, of course, an eczema breakout.

In the early days of my schooling, I dreaded having the conversation at home about how to give the authorities the information they sought without telling our "family bit-ness." My mother had gotten pregnant in her freshman year at Norfolk State by a "Black street hustler from Baltimore," then took another man's name and left for Detroit with breastmilk in tow. Neither of them, out of the three, wanted me, so I was left behind for my maternal grandparents to raise straight from the hospital. My mother's new military man vehemently denied that I could be his when I came out because, after all, I didn't meet the color test with skin so brown that I couldn't be his child. He was as light as my biological mother. It was only enough to stop them from fussing about my mother's lifestyle choices. My grandparents stepped in and up because that is what grandparents in the Black community do; it raised the second generation of children without flinchin'. A call of duty. A labor of love. I shudder to think where we would be in this world as a people without the passion and commitment of our grandparents.

NEVER SAID A WORD

The way my grandparents would say the word Black when they described my biological father, I could tell they were disgusted. As much as they loved me, I was still the black sheep, a dark horse in a family in denial about being somewhat color-struck. I believed that as much as they loved me, they were raising the product of something they despised most—a dark-skinned Black man. My grandmother was not as verbal in front of me, as much as my grandfather. My grandfather said things like, "That no good Black nigga," this. And, "That no good Black nigga," referencing his daughters, my aunt, and mother, "they'... try to get to his daughters just want'em mess with'em cause the way they look." I took it as light-skinned. My mother was just as fair as my grandmother, and her sister, my aunt, who was like a big sister to me, was the spitting image of my grandmother. Each of them could pass for white if they wanted to. They each embodied the term 'redbone' through and through. They had no brown paper bag test issues. My uncle, who I looked to as my older brother, had a redness in his skin tone that revealed his Native glow with his father's skin.

The thing is, I looked more like the kids in the house across the street from us than I did my own family. They were all foster children that I enjoyed playing with often. There was Marie and Mike, who everyone called Woogie, and Carl, who was the big, mean one. I remember one day playing with Marie on our porch when my godmother, Sonja, was visiting. During that time, she worked with the state as a counselor for truant kids. She'd show up wearing a lanyard with her badges and credentials swinging in motion against her beautifully suited frame. She was the only person in my life who visited me often, and with each visit, I felt special. She was solely there for me and had a way of making me feel unique. Approaching the front door, she'd always be holding something in her hands with my name on it—often a small token of some kind, usually a half-dollar or one-dollar coin.

Marie once asked me who my godmother was after she left. I explained it was my godmother, but she laughed and said, "Nah-

ah, she yo' case worker. I got one, and she looks like a case worker."
Her words planted a seed of doubt in my mind about my very own
existence. I wondered if she was right. I had already compared my
skin tone and hair texture to those of my immediate family, and
there wasn't a match. Then I compared them to the woman,
"supposed to be my mother," and thought, *You know, maybe Marie
is right!* So, I began the deep dive, looking intensely through every
tattered family photo album I could get my little hands on. It
bothered me so badly that I became obsessed with knowing the
truth.

Desperate for answers, I finally asked my grandmother if I
was a foster child. She laughed in a way I had never heard her laugh
before. It was infectious. I even laughed with her briefly, although
the exchange frightened me. I didn't know whether she was
genuinely amused or lightening the moment to break some bad
news. After she finished cackling and crackin' up, however, she
said, "No baby–you are not a foster child. Where in the hell did you
get something like that from?" I explained how.

"Marie said, 'Momma Sonja looks like a case worker," I
said. She laughed again. I must admit, for a while, I still thought she
might be lying in an attempt not to hurt my feelings. I was coming
to an age when you couldn't tell me anything. In my mind, it had to
make sense. I was already insecure about who I was. There wasn't
much uncertainty that I could take.

It wasn't until I discovered my birth certificate that my
doubts were eased. Unfortunately, it was precisely then that my
insecurities grew. Once I knew who my birth mother was, I wanted
to know everything about her. The number of questions flying
through my head wouldn't let me rest until I landed on an
explanation for why she was letting her parents do the hard work of
raising me. All I knew was that it must have been something due to
my skin color.

I must have gone through every single photo in the house. I mean hundreds of pictures. I was looking for a picture that would connect me to her. What was peculiar was that I could not find one picture of my mother holding me or my hand as an infant or toddler. I wondered if we had ever had a genuine connection in the first place. When visiting relatives, I found pictures of my grandmother holding me as an infant, dated October 1964, in Richmond, Virginia. I saw pictures of my grandparents helping me to walk when I was a few years older. I found one picture of my mother sitting beside me on the porch. I was holding a ball that I seemed pretty excited about. But not one picture ever showed her hugging me, kissing me, not even touching me, nothing. Not one. During my abandonment recovery, Susan Anderson's book "The Journey from Abandonment to Healing," regarding the chapter on Unfinished Business From The Past, The Abandoned Child Within, explains the function of the locus ceruleus (LC) located in the brainstem. I learned it plays a crucial role in the connection or disconnection of the physiological and cognitive functions. Research shows that newborn animals who are separated from their mothers show a change in the structure and function of their LC. This study is related to humans. Even in brief periods, interrupted bonds have lifelong effects on the brain. The change is not subtle but a significant change that can leave that crucial organ underdeveloped. It can also leave it less productive of norepinephrine, inhibiting hyperalertness and contributing to anxiety and depression. At that time, I understood that my hardwiring had been shortened.

I was about six years old when I first saw my mother and truly understood who she was to me. She came into the house wearing a maxi-length coat—a multi-colored one with a wide black faux-fur band at the base, wrist, and collar. She was wearing that coat! It had a nice Russian flare that made it look straight from the runways in Paris and Milan. As much as I was in awe of her fashion sense and hazel eyes (that matched my grandfather's), I stood behind my grandmother's coattails and resisted the interaction.

FONDA E. WOODARD

One Christmas, my mother gave me a baby doll that looked identical to her, right down to the hairstyle and her outfit for the times. The doll was about a foot and a half long with a beautiful, multi-colored dress and had the nerve to have heels. I called it "Dessa Doll," aptly named after its giver. I resented that doll when she placed it in my hands. When I was alone, I would scold the doll's face as if it were my mother's, asking pressing questions that I would dare not deliver to the real version of Momma Dessa. "Why did you come here?" "Why did you leave me?" "Why can't I live with you?" "Why can't I be with you?" I'd quietly scream, knowing the doll was mute and thus without a valid way of defending itself. I'd often find myself pinching at the porcelain-colored skin covering that little plastic body, hoping she could feel the pain I felt over my mother's abandonment. "You can't even talk. Ugggggggggghhhh!" Finally, after I realized there were no answers to be given or satisfaction to be gained, I'd throw the doll into the corner out of frustration. No answers. Just like the real thing. Think Bobo doll experiment.

For much of my childhood, I felt powerless and unworthy of attention, thus acting out. The deep emotional wounds that stemmed from my looks and how I grew to understand my identity were hot, tender, and raw for a long, long time. I would eventually learn to embrace my natural curls and coils and find ways to deal with my eczema breakouts. Finally, I wanted my grandparents to release their preconceived notions of dark-skinned people that they didn't even realize were influencing how they acted around me and not just to love me because I was theirs. But to genuinely love all color like mine. The one thing I desired most but never got was my mother's unconditional love. The kind of internalized pain sat on my chest like an elephant. Suffocation implodes.

CHAPTER 2

North Star

I love that I grew up in a working-class neighborhood. There was a culture about North Newport News that I can't help but think of fondly whenever I reminisce. North Newport News wasn't at the bottom of the class, nor were we at the top of the class structure. As a little girl, I thought ALL people who lived uptown were rich, and people who lived downtown were poor, thinking your affluence was based on location, living off Jefferson Avenue. As I grew, I learned every section within each zip code had various levels of affluence, most were hard-working, and everyone was trying to make their way in life.

Those working for the military or Shipbuilding and Dry Dock would come home filthy from a hard day's work. By late afternoon, they'd have spent most of the day pulling miles of cables inside aircraft carriers or ships. Or metal workers dusty from performing their skilled work in whatever destroyer they were working on. That's the kind of stuff we do in Newport News. We build shit! We have built the best of the best by the best for generations. If it's out somewhere floating and defending this nation in the name of the Department of Defense, particularly the Navy, foreign and domestic, it likely came through Newport News Shipbuilding. That Coats & Clark zippers and Coca-Cola StarrX bottle openers. If you know, you know. It was work that generations upon generations of families have had their hands in and on, of which they should be proud. I know I am.

The hands of Newport News' community members can tell generational stories of dedication and perseverance. The calluses, the scars, the burns, the minor cuts, the nasty scrapes, and yes, the sickness of asbestos all speak to the sacrifice of the community that continues to flourish throughout those 120 square miles of the city. As a military vet, it feels like a full-circle moment to witness. I am proud to know that people from my hometown and my neighborhood have had a hands-on opportunity to manage the most sophisticated vessels the rest of the country has relied on for centuries. Remembering the blood of many people who've sacrificed and built remarkable national defense vessels for millions and staked their lives so we have our freedoms is a beautiful thought. We may be a small town, but we're mighty, made up of an ingenious population of folks who understand the meaning and value behind hard work. Growing up in the '60s and '70s, this notion was on full display as I took to it more quickly than many young girls my age usually did. Watching the people in my community make an honest living to provide for their families by working for their country made me want a good-paying government job instead of pursuing modeling or acting like some friends said they wanted to do. I said as much when I was competing in the Miss Black Teenage World competition at the Moton Theatre back in the day.

The way people would strive for better back then made Christmastime in my neighborhood much more enjoyable. It was the time of the year when you could recognize the attitude of working hard and playing hard that many adults possessed. All the older men who lived there, like my granddaddy and some of his friends, would be so busy throughout the year that this was the time they'd get to go to each other's houses, relax, enjoy each other's company, and be at peace with the quality time spent. Most of this quality time culminated in their 'drunk walk', like a neighborhood beer crawl. Except instead of beer, there was eggnog and a couple of shots of liquor at one person's place and then more at another until they'd downed about a whole bottle together by the end of the night. Outside of the holidays, some people would sell the same shots of liquor to whoever came knocking for a small price. We had two shot houses in our neighborhood, Peter Rabbits and Bozo's. They called them 'shot' houses because you could go there and buy a shot of liquor when you couldn't afford the whole bottle. We had two neighborhood spots, like the T.V. show back in the '80s, called "Cheers." Our neighborhood bars were Jones' Paradise and The Purple Rainbow, also known as Bae & Pugs Place. Some considered them holes in the wall, but they were respectable businesses and important to the culture of North Newport News because they were owned and operated by neighbors. And it was a place *"where everybody knew your name, and they're always glad you came!"* just like the show's theme song. At Christmas, when the giving spirit of the season would render the shot houses almost useless, I'd watch the neighborhood men carry out their annual ritual for as long as I was allowed because when grown folks were talking in the room, there was no hanging around. They send you away saying, "Go'on now, grown folks talkin'." Meanwhile, their wives would sit, chat, and spend time with Ma and me in another part of the house.

The best part of our neighborhood was that it was full of kids. The worst was that I grew up an only child, so having kids my age with whom to play was nice. Other kids had siblings. I only had stupid dolls. Our streets were lined with ditches filled with tadpoles, crayfish, bullfrogs, and worms, and I can still remember playing with friends as the hot sun rose high in the Virginia sky. We'd play kickball and dodgeball, too. I would love to throw and kick the football in the streets until the streetlights came on and it was time to go inside. Or until the shipyard whistle blew, whichever mattered more at the moment. We had the occasional sighting of the Purple Lady, a.k.a. Ms. Rachel Amelia Presha. The local Peninsula urban legend was known for her purple-colored hair, clothing, shopping cart, and house. She lived "cross the water" in Suffolk. Presha died in 2017 at age 91. God bless her. She entertained us for sure!

The shipyard whistle sounds like the city of Newport News' alarm clock. You can set your watch by it. It alerts employees to the start and end of the shifts and lunch breaks. When the end-of-the-day whistle blew at 3:30 p.m., everybody knew it was quitting time for more than 16,000 employees, mommas, and daddies to come home. If you were a child of a parent who worked in the shipyard and were given a list of chores to do, once that whistle blew, that list better be complete. If not, you'd better run home, sweatin' bullets formed across your forehead, gettin' it done before they crossed the threshold.

I remember wanting nothing more than to feel like I belonged in those days. Coincidentally, I felt most at home with the foster kids who lived across the street from us, Marie and her brothers Carl and Woogie. The four of us were practically crabs in the same pot. The only difference was how we'd gotten there in the first place. I might've ended up with my blood relatives, but each had been somewhat abandoned.

I would play with Marie, Woogie, and Carl every day outside in our yards. Marie was my favorite, but I liked Woogie too because I always felt like he was calm in the middle of the storm. The elders would say Carl was 'bitten by a mean streak.' He had a terrible attitude, I assume, like most older teenagers caught up in the foster care system. He was a bully, full stop—big, tall, loud and intimidating. Sometimes, I'd think he'd spit to disgust people since he did it so much. For no good, apparent reason, he was just nasty. He'd push his younger siblings around, literally and figuratively, and now and again, he'd lose his temper over something small and take it out on the people around him. If he weren't winning in a board game, he'd get up and flip the board so none of us could play. Woogie always wanted to play fair, and he was the only person I knew who could diffuse Carl's destructive behaviors.

The Wilsons lived two doors down from Marie. They had seven kids, with two of them being twins; they were more of a clan to me. There were so many of them that they tended to keep to themselves. The two oldest kids were kind of 'standoff-ish' to me, but it was because I was a little kid to them. The age range in their family was vast. Some of them were very nice and sweet, others not so lovely. I'd be so desperate to be their friend and in their company that I would endure any behavior they choose to deal with me on any given day. I distinctly recall one time during one of their family cookouts when they had a blanket party. They were tossing the little kids around on the blankets, but when my turn came, they beat and kicked my ass as if I had stolen something. It was like an old-fashioned military blanket party—the one where they released the Kraken on me. I went from being happy in a familial setting, eating food, and listening to music to lying on the ground in pain after being mercilessly kicked and punched. Once they were done, I realized they didn't want me there with them, not on that day nor in that setting. I was not welcomed. I was sent home with more than a bruised body but black and blue feelings.

What bothered me the most about that incident was that no one in the group ever said a word. I don't know if their mother knew. All I knew was no one said that was wrong. Mrs. Wilson was different. She kept to herself; though she spoke, she could sometimes be off-putting. She was strict and always ensured her kids kept their home clean. Whenever I was over there, I was cleaning with them. I was happy to do it as long as I was with some friends. They were good people.

Living just up the street from me was Karen, a pretty little brown girl I played with who had sickle cell anemia. I loved playing with her. She was funny and had a quick wit. I liked that she never wanted you to feel sorry for her. She was different, but that only meant she needed to be loved differently, which was no other story than any of us. I learned about this concept of love from her, and I've never forgotten it. The neighborhood was full of little blockhead boys, the Clark, Maddox, and Lockhart boys, who seemed to "*pick*" on me. But the only little boy who toted my book bag home was named Terrence, whose nickname was Bay-Bay. He lived on Lyndon Circle. He was a sweet little brown boy with a big blockhead and a broad smile. We had the best time growing up in our North Newport News neighborhood. It was filled with kids and was vibrant with life.

If I couldn't hang out with Marie and her brothers or play with Karen or the Wilsons, then Judy was the closest thing I had to a friend. The neighbors lived in the house adjacent to ours, on the opposite corner of Center and Swan, and they always had junk lying around the inside and outside of their home. It was a lot of junk, enough to be both a child's utopia and an OSHA fire hazard, all wrapped in one, especially with the stacks of old papers and magazines lined up and down the hall posing as a collection.

Judy and I would spend our time playing board games at her house. At that time, it wasn't common for children to play inside each other's houses. Most adults didn't want their living spaces turned upside down to make way for hide and seek and other games. But on cold days or rainy summer afternoons, Judy's parents would allow us to play inside the addition they'd built onto the side of their house. She'd invite her two brothers to sit at the restaurant-style booth they had in there. Gary would pull out the games and sit at the table, with Judy and Gary on one side and me and her younger brother Donald on the other. You know how the hairs on the back of your neck start to rise at the slightest feeling that something ain't right? That is what Donald brought over me during those moments of what should've been innocent play. After a while, I stopped wanting to go over there when he kept trying to touch and grab between my legs whenever we sat beside each other.

Stuck inside the booth, I would inch closer and closer to the wall to get away from him, but the longer it went on, the worse it got. I was too young to understand what was happening then, but I knew how uncomfortable it made me feel. I was sure that Judy and Gary could see everything, but they never said a word about it. After a while, the whole situation became so stressful that I stopped spending time in the neighbor's house. If it weren't nice enough to play outside in the open on fair weather days, I wouldn't play. It was at that time that Judy indeed became my fair-weather friend. But soon, I could barely call her that.

The neighbors belonged to a "walkie-talkie" club, a group of people who were Citizens Band (CB) radio fanatics. The CB communication system is a short-distance, person-to-person radio ordinarily used in a fixed location, similar to those used on the road by long-distance truck drivers or police officers. However, the neighbors and their white friends used it from home to home like a telephone party line. Pre-cable television and the remote control, their past-time fun was the neighborhood's most significant nuisance. Back then, all we had was our rabbit ear antennas sitting on the top of the TV to get reception.

On the other hand, the neighbor's CB system required mounts and cable holders, beams, and shit! At least it looked space-age, like something from the Jetsons cartoon. Half the time, we didn't know what to think of its presence. All anybody knew when the thing was operating was that no TV in the hood could get a clear picture.

My granddaddy would get so mad that he'd get on the landline, call over to their house, and cuss Mr. Jimmie out as soon as he picked up the phone. "Listen, man," he'd start. "You need to cut that shit out. It's fuckin' up everybody's TV." That phrase and hearing the words expressed like that, my little mind repeated, *"fuckin' up?' Now that's a word—I like it!'"* The colossal antenna perched on their detached garage to sharpen the CB signal looked like a gigantic wishbone, and our house sat closest to it. At the time, our region only had about five channels altogether. Three of them were the significant VHF channels—3, 10, and 13, still in existence today. The other two were UHF minor channels, 27 and 33. But TV channels didn't come in clear when Mr. Jimmie and his friends talked on those shortwaves.

The CB club members were primarily white folks living in the New Market area who were no more than one or two generations removed from being considered poor white trash, at best. They also happened to be overt racists and known bigots, but that never stopped the neighbors from socializing with them. With her fair skin, straight hair, and hazel eyes, Judy looked more like my grandparents and relatives in North Carolina than I did. On the other hand, her father was a short, bald, brown-skinned man who served in the Navy. I'm still not sure of how he was able to fit in with that crowd of overt racist white people said to hate our kind so much. Most of the time, I would have been long gone when they showed up for his get-togethers. On one particular occasion, I guess I didn't leave soon enough for Mr. Jimmie's satisfaction.

It had only been about 10, maybe 15 minutes after I'd gotten over there when Judy told me her dad said I had to leave and go back home. Confused, I asked why since we had just begun to play. Before she could sugarcoat it, her father answered, "'Cause you too dark to be here playing with Judy. I got my friends coming over here. Go'on on and take your black ass home."

First, he had NEVER talked to me like that, if he said anything at all. But at that moment, his words cut like a knife. It reinforced every insecurity, every wound, every ill-mended scar that was already going on in my heart, mind, and within the four walls of my family's home. I said we were all color-struck back then, but this was me learning how he felt about me. And with his teeth gritted, he leaned into my face, and it was clear. Yes, it is a fact and phenomenon that I witnessed with my own eyes in my neighborhood—dark-skinned men loving fair-skinned women, and it seemed that fair-skinned women loved some dark-skinned men. I likened it to what I later learned was some sick cultural trophy spouse syndrome. The way I saw it, men viewed their women through a lens of understanding that the lighter, the better. Then, more women viewed their men through a similar focus of the darker, the better. It seemed most Black men desired a Lena Horne over a Nina Simone. Was dark skin in? Or was it dark out? Was light in, or was light out? The '70s were so confusing for me.

To make things worse, my grandfather wasn't the type who initially welcomed brown-skinned men into the lives of his daughters either. He had no problem with most people knowing it on the basic level. That was at least before I came along. He didn't know how to love color. I taught him that lesson of love.

My uncle used to call me chocolate, my favorite flavor of ice cream. One day, while thoroughly enjoying a double scoop of my favorite, he'd said, "If I kept eating chocolate ice cream, I would continue to get darker." I was a kid; I didn't know he was joking. But my eating behavior changed after that. I began to faithfully eat plain vanilla ice cream only because I wanted to be fair-skinned like the rest of the family. He said that if I ate vanilla, I would get as light as him and my aunt Tina. When I began to miss my old favorite flavor, I decided to eat the chocolate/vanilla swirl instead. I figured I'd get a taste of what I loved most without compromising my complexion. Believe it or not, the little things said to me as a child most impacted my overall thinking and self-esteem, even if it was meant as a joke. Things such as these developed a hard mass in my throat that felt more like a fist. Often, my eyes immediately swelled and filled with tears of defeat.

I ran out of the neighbor's house so fast after Mr. Jimmie said those mean things to me. I don't think I'd ever run any quicker. My feet propelled me directly into the arms of my grandmother. As soon as I saw her, I grabbed onto her waist and thrust my head into her lap. I was crying my eyes out so badly I could hardly speak when she asked me what happened. "Are you hurt?" she wondered as she hung up the phone. She'd just been laughing with my Uncle Bump's wife, Aunt Doll. All she could do was frantically search my eyes for some answer. All I could do was shake my head, 'No.' But the story spilled out once she straightened my back and calmed me down.

Sniffling as I could hardly speak, "Mr. Jimmie didn't want his friends to see me playing with Judy because I was too dark to play with her. He told me to take my black ass home," I said.

Those words sighted my grandmother's rage; her eyes grew as big as a silver dollar, and her fair skin turned ghost-white. "He said, WHAAAAT?!" she exclaimed. She was fish grease hot! Snatching my arm up my right elbow in one hand, she chicken-winged me, scooped my narrow ass on my toes, and together we marched out the back door to my granddaddy's shed. "COME ON," she said as we headed out the back door. As soon as the back screen door slammed shut, she hollered, "Odellllllll!" We found him tinkering around in his shed like he'd typically done—cutting on this and fixing on that. My grandmother nudged me to tell him the story. "Go on, tell'em what Jimmie said to you."

You could always tell when my dad was pissed off because the color of his hazel eyes would change to a yellowish-golden brown from the blood rushing to them. When his eyes changed color, we'd know all hell was coming. When I finished telling the story for a second time, he saw how upset my grandmother and I were. I saw ALL hell coming.

Without saying a word, he took his time pulling his handkerchief out of his back pocket and wiping off the oil on his hands. Then he wiped across his forehead and the rest of his face. Finally, he said, "Y'all go back in the house," and put his dirty handkerchief back in his pocket.

Letting the back door slam behind us, we went to the back bedroom window where we could peep at him through the slits in the metal blinds. Next thing we knew, my daddy called Mr. Jimmie up to the side of the chain link fence, gesturing for him to talk. "Jimmie," he remarked as he waved a motion to come. Somewhat annoyed because he had company, Mr. Jimmie anxiously approached the edge of the chain link fence. But before he could get a single word out, my granddaddy snatched him up and across the chain links that separated our properties. He then laid his ass straight out on the freshly tilled dirt in his garden. With one fist filled with Mr. Jimmie's shirt collar and the other in front of his face, he said, "Don't you ever talk to my granddaughter like that again, you hear me? Don't you evah tell my granddaughter she ain't good enough to play witchyo' daughter again! I will beat your ass and bury you in this goddamn garden. Don't mess with me, I don't play that shit!" He snatched him back off the ground, helped him to his feet, brushed the dirt off his back, and pushed him on his way. "Now get the fuck off my property."

Mr. Jimmie had to walk back around the fence to get to his white friends who continued to sit under his garage and driveway port. I wondered if they were too shocked or passive about what had just occurred to attempt to intervene. I knew they didn't want any smoke from that chimney because that Odell fire was hot!

After that, via the Richardson family executive order, I was forbidden to play with Judy from that day on, no matter how fair the weather was. It had been clear that she could play in our yard, but I was never to step foot in hers again.

That was the day I learned two things. One, my affinity for the word "fuck" and two, how my daddy's protective nature could be swift and unforgiving. It taught me to be careful when sharing information about those who would hurt me. Mostly, I was scared because I loved my grandfather so much I never wanted anything to happen to him. He was the only father I'd ever known. I worried that if he lost his temper, he might hurt or kill somebody over something they'd done to me. I was thinking, *If he did that to Mr. Jimmie, with white folks nearby, there's no telling what he would do in a worse situation. What would he do if he ever found out how Donald would fiddle with me whenever I was over their house on cold and rainy days? I don't want him to lose his good government job.* It's because of incidents like this that I began repressing emotions of shame and holding secrets that have stayed with me until now. With few friends to confide in, I felt I had to find ways to cope with the struggle of finding myself in a world that didn't seem to want me all that much. That struggle only intensified as I grew older and spent more time in my birth mother's care. And the battle was real.

CHAPTER 3

Identity Crisis

L ater in life, through therapy, I learned that some of my earliest childhood memories are not exactly forgotten. They are simply unreachable. In Mark Wolynn's "It Didn't Start With You," I learned that most of us carry residue from our family history that we know nothing about. Some things we inherit are not written in wills, testaments, or trusts. They are aspects of trauma that are a shared family biological consciousness. As much as I might think with my rational mind that I may not feel some way about some of the things that happened to me as a child, my body continues to remember—pushing itself through the world as if it's still being weighed down by all the baggage my brain wants so badly to move away from carousel number one, me. Only in adulthood did I learn how suppressed trauma affected my central nervous system and the effects it would have on my life for decades to come.

One of the most significant lessons I learned in abandonment therapy was "A Mini Lesson on the Emotional Brain," as explained by Susan Anderson in her book, "The Journey from Abandonment to Healing." I learned how the amygdala plays a central role in emotionally responding. Functioning as the body's central alarm system, it scans for any possible threat, be it emotional or physical, but especially for anything that recalls a previous fear-laden experience. When the amygdala detects a problem, it declares an emotional emergency and sets off an emotional crisis. As we grow, the amygdala continuously gathers memories of how we've responded to fear and other perceived threats since infancy. These emotional memories help us detect dangers we've learned about from previous experiences, both as a species (don't step over the edge of a cliff) and individually (don't go near Uncle Fathead). It is also believed to contain traces of our prenatal and birth experiences. But once the amygdala has been conditioned to an emotional response (i.e., feeling anxious when a loved one threatens separation), its learning is nearly indelible. "In other words, when it comes to emotional memory, the slate never gets 'completely' wiped clean" (Anderson, 2000).

When I learned of the indelible emotional residue left behind like watermarks on a page, I yelled, "INFANCY!" Psychiatrist Thomas Verny further explains in his book, "Nurturing the Unborn Child: A Nine-Month Program for Soothing, Stimulating, and Communicating with Your Baby," that pregnant women's bodies will manufacture stress hormones, adrenaline, and noradrenaline, that will travel through both the mother's bloodstream introducing stress on both mother and child. Those studies showed that under extreme and constant stress, mothers are more likely to have premature babies, low birth weights, colicky, and hyperactive. Avoiding stress is nothing new to mothers who have always been told to 'manage your stress' while pregnant. But often, we find it easier to say than do. I didn't know how that stress leaves indelible marks on your child.

Understanding there is a scientific explanation for the issues between me and my mother allowed me to experience deeper self-compassion and compassion for her. My thoughts surrounding nature versus nurture took on a different meaning. Our experiences, environments, and social groups all influence who we are and how we operate. Only after I went through therapy as an adult was I fully able to recognize how deeply my past traumas had affected every thought, decision, and move that I'd made up until that point. And it had all affected me before I was even born. I could not help but think, if this is my true story, what is my mother's true story?

My mother and I were never able to connect or communicate productively. I never understood why it was so difficult when I was young. My body knew the truth, and it responded in kind. I could always sense how this young vessel of mine was rejected. The more she exhibited neglectful behavior, the more awkward things became, creating a deeper divide she could not traverse to develop an authentic and meaningful relationship with me.

In the era I was born into, pre-Roe v. Wade, women didn't have safe access to alternative health care if they found themselves with an unwanted pregnancy. Many women, particularly women of color, would die on the table trying to make their way to the other side of backdoor abortions. Back then, it was more feasible to grit your teeth and raise multiple children or let aunts and uncles raise them in another state if they had to as if to hide the truth. I do not doubt that my mother had no advantage over other options, safe or otherwise. I may not be here telling this story had she been afforded the post-Roe benefit of choice. To have, raise, or otherwise deal with an unwanted pregnancy had to be frightening. It was just a sign of the times. Yet here we are again with NO CHOICE for women. It is almost difficult to believe. In many ways, my mother was also a victim. The world would make her think it was of her own volition, but the truth is, no one knows how she was affected by the things that transpired in her young life. Her voice has been silenced by trauma, too.

I don't know the emotional detriment my mother experienced when my grandmother was caring for her in the womb. Nor do I know what my grandmother was going through during pregnancy with my mother. The degree to which my mother was affected by grief and fear over the unexpected loss of her siblings, stillborn during childbirth, shaped her in incalculable ways, leaving indelible marks of her own. I don't know how hard it has been to navigate life with one eye from adolescence through adulthood and into her senior years. I know she must have felt alone and afraid as a child, changing the trajectory of her life. As life would have it, I imagine those same emotions revisited her soon after graduating high school. She experienced abandonment by the man whom she loved and was supposed to have loved her back, only to vanish without a trace, leaving her with a child. That is a compounded predicament with life-altering implications that are truly unimaginable.

My mother doesn't possess those maternal instincts due to the compound effect of her trauma. So, as it was, I'm sure there was no nurturing me during pregnancy. It is even less likely we listened to music while in utero. Even more doubtful, she talked to me quietly, reading while dreaming of my face and rubbing her belly. And I understand why. I am not naïve to think those instincts existed before I was conceived. That is what trauma does: it is a thief, robbing and wreaking emotional havoc. I believe it stole my mother's maternal instincts before they stood a chance to develop. As a mother myself, I have cried for the little girl inside me who never asked to be placed in this world yet expected to endure all the cruelties that came from that lack of early connection. I needed to understand the pain of abandonment to provide hope for future generations.

Sadness and isolation were a complex cocktail of pills to swallow. The pain of trying to sustain my mother's attention to no avail would feel like wearing a weighted vest while swimming. I'd look at her and think, is this what women do? I'd ask myself, *is this how women act? Is this what motherhood is 'supposed' to be, and is this how a mother should act?* A lot of times, I questioned my mother's capacity to love anyone, including herself. It was then I understood not to take this shit personally, but it wasn't easy. This was never about me but, instead, about her. I cannot imagine the pain in her untold story.

Often, I'd wonder why she wasn't more like her sister. My aunt was different. And though she was my aunt, Tina was more like the older sister I looked up to and aspired to be like. She is the one I grew up with in the home where my grandparents raised us. She was the best thing in my life when I was younger. Like her, I wanted a college education and a good government job. I admired her intelligence and independence. She went to Hampton University in Virginia, back when it was still called Hampton Institute. She'd get books from the library and bring them home for me to read. "Green Eggs and Ham" by Dr. Suess was the first one. I still have the copy. I always read it to her so frequently that when I read it to my grandkids now, remembering that innocent time in my youth brings joy to my heart. To my Aunt Tina, I was an empty vessel, and whenever there was time, she had no problem pouring in the love and attention I so desperately needed. She was always getting me into developmental activities. That's one of the main ways she showed me care and love. Just showing up was all I needed. Together, we were the definition of busybodies–always on the go. You could hardly pin us down to one activity. My affinity for ballet originated with Aunt Tina when she signed me up for classes. Then, it became regular trips to Hilton off Main Street for lessons in the upstairs studio.

  In contrast, my mother's decision to leave outweighed her only reason to stay: me. The absence resulted in missed milestones, such as my first lost tooth, my first day at school at every level, and my first crush. You get it. She left me behind and moved from Virginia to Detroit, seemingly without a second thought, with breastmilk in tow. As a mother with hindsight, I know the importance of skin-to-skin contact and the superpower of breast milk. I didn't realize how much a lack of both would affect us. I never got an opportunity for any of that type of physical connection to listen to my mother's heartbeat or feel the warmth of her skin's temperature. She never intended to have her only daughter join her on the move. I know a lot of it had to do with my grandfather. He was the kind of man you didn't want to cross. If he said, "You're not going to take this child with you to Detroit," the discussion was over. The things you learn when you get older bring a clear perspective. The fact remains that my mother's choice was not to stay with me in Newport News either. There was no sense of obligation to provide that early connection and essential nutritional requisite needed for growth at that tender stage of life. She decided to go to Detroit instead of mothering her only newborn girl child. That was the most painful fact to realize.

Feelings of abandonment cut deep as the layers of a cesarean. Yet I was still expected to have some semblance of a relationship with a mother who seemed to have cared less. As a little girl, before I started school, my grandparents would shove the phone in my face, rushing me into speaking in an unrecognizable voice on the other end. Then I'd freeze, unsure of what to do or what to say, not knowing who was really on the other end of the line or what connection I had to them. Back then, calling people long distance wasn't something that happened daily. Long-distance phone calls were expensive. You could only stay on and talk for a few minutes at a time, so I'd be rushed into starting a conversation, and quickly, as they rushed to speak, the phone was taken away because you couldn't waste phone time. My mama (grandma) and daddy (granddaddy) sat beside me. Everyone I knew in my nuclear family, including my brother, Lewis, and my sister, Tina, was there. So, who could this stranger be? I rarely had anything to say except for "hi" because I was told not to talk to strangers.

Once I started putting the puzzle pieces together, maybe the voice on the phone was my older aunt, my mother's sister. I was in a constant state of confusion about who my mother was and what she was supposed to be to me. My confidence level immediately began to plummet. As I matured, I constantly sought validation and connection in spaces where I would neither receive nor benefit from the relationships that were supposed to foster it. It never occurred to me that it would begin at home and extend into other environments where I didn't feel happy or with people who didn't add value to my life. And, no matter the hurt, I would still feel a desire to stay locked in, to lose myself in relationships or activities because, for whatever reason, that is where I found comfort. I wanted to feel seen and heard, but most of all, I wanted to be liked by my mother, even if she could not show me. That became my desired goal concerning my mother–but it turned into my Achilles heel. More appropriately, it was like a weed of desperation growing through a cement crack caused by my mother's lack of involvement and engagement. As I grew, that weed continued to grow and take over our relationship like a sidewalk of a path less traveled. Her resistance to engage permitted weeds to eventually bury the entire path's foundation as an unrecognizable route and indefinitely change the direction of our mother-daughter route.

As an adolescent little girl, my godmother constantly told me, "That's just who she is, baby. The sooner you accept your mother for who she is, the less you'll take it personally. She has treated everyone who cared about her the same way." I was well into my 50s before I realized Sonja's advice and heed her warnings. Once I truly understood my mother's capabilities, my stressors were minimized. I stopped seeking a deeper relationship with her, like mine and my grandmother's. My grandmother has always been Momma to me, not her daughter, which is why it was so shocking to my system to hear my birth mother respond to "Ma" for the first time.

I had to be about 8 or 9 years old when I called out "Ma" one day in a family group setting, expecting to hear my grandmother respond, and my mother answered instead. As quick as I listened to the words leave her lips, my head spun like a horror flick, and I stared out of confusion. Sayin' to myself, *I know YO ass ain't answering to MA!* And–yes, I thought that foul language in my head at that early age because Houston, we got a problem! My brain was yelling, over and over, *She is NOT MA! She is NOT MA! She is NOT MA!* But she still answered naturally as if she was.

Then I realized she had an audience and she was on stage. From then on, I called her Mama Dessa only to delineate the difference between the two exclusively. I used the name often enough to remind her of her ranking in position to my real Ma. The one who'd been caring for me during her sabbatical. The one who had been with me when I was happy, sad, or sick. The real Ma that was the first nurse, the first doctor, and the first teacher! My head was pounding so hard at times with thoughts of how she abandoned me that I could not sleep. My thoughts of how she had left me straight out of the hospital or insisted that we live in separate homes consumed me. I believed the woman had lost her mind and was thoroughly confused about the role she chose to have in my life. *Stop the performance, prodigal daughter!*

For a long time, I felt my mother's sole purpose was to create constant confusion. She always had this passive-aggressive way of dealing with me. We never talked—ever. I cannot remember one significant conversation that didn't end in an argument. Even when she moved back in with us at our house for a short stint, I realized that we could never be like those other mother-daughter duos that spent much time together, connecting through conversation and experiences. By the time I made it to the fourth grade, all I had hoped was for us to develop a relationship that would ease my emotional hunger for her attention. But I was denied at every turn. Every year I grew older, her lack of trying made me angrier. And what exasperated the pain was the reliving and dissociation of the trauma that occurred every time I was with her. The thoughts, sounds, and emotions of it all became serial flashbacks in quick motion, and I wanted to die so that she would be left with unbearable pain.

Although I stayed with Mama Dessa on and off while she was married to Al, she persistently resisted having any deep emotional engagement with me. One of the most intimate moments I evoked was baking cookies. Even then, she would make it painfully clear with every single decision and move that she was uninterested in taking on her role as a full-time mother. A small but significant example of how she operated outside of herself was when baking cookies. Baking cookies wasn't something she'd excitedly announce as our thing. It was just something that she'd planned to do over the weekends. She would be baking cookies every weekend, especially around the holidays anyway. She'd start pulling out her flour, baking powder, baking soda, etc., and I would join her. Then, when she'd box them to share with family and friends, she'd never say, "Me and Fonda baked these." Instead, she'd say here are some cookies I baked this weekend. Sometimes I just wanted to say, 'Damn, you know I was there, right?' She'd become so accustomed to leaving me out that even when I was there and involved, it was natural to leave me out.

Yet, the whole time, I was just trying to please her. I wanted to learn how to bake, measure the mixture, and form perfect shapes that weren't deformed or burnt. I just wanted her to like me, even if she couldn't love me. At times, the tolerance she showed me was enough for me to get by. Honestly, I didn't know what love would look like from her for a long time, and in many ways, I still don't. The key to my mental well-being is managing my emotions this season, which is boundary management. Nevertheless, I prayed to be the kind of little girl she would favor, hoping to earn her time and affection because I felt empty without it. I was sure that, in some aspects, she might have felt that same emptiness, and if given a chance, it would benefit us both.

Understanding my capabilities in mothering my two girls broadened my perspective and liberated my mindset about my mother and her capacity to love. What was reflective for me was the era we were in, the availability of a suitable support system, and God's immense grace and mercy. For each of us, it was a tale of two different times. What made it even more difficult for her was the fact that I was too much like the man who lied to her about his intentions and left her with a child. My skin was dark — just like his. I had that same little dimple in the middle of my chin, you know, that dominant allele cleft chin that comes from the male gene? Yes, I got one, just like my biological father's. The older I got, the more my quick tongue clapped back in response to her lack of accountability. And yes, I inherited that gift of gab quick tongue from him, too. Just like him, I had a badass Baltimore attitude and the hustle of a survivor of the fittest. I understand how spending time with me could be painful and cause Post Traumatic Stress Disorder (PTSD) triggers for her, laden with disdain for me. I also understand that, in some respects, it still has the same effect. It reminds me that my mother, too, is hurting from a traumatic past she so desperately wants to leave behind.

The first time I recognized our emotional disconnection was when we were out somewhere together with my grandmother. My grandmother was in another aisle, and I stood with my mother. A random woman noted my beauty. I was very young then and couldn't have been over 8 years old, as this was around 1974. Suddenly, a stranger standing nearby refers to me as a *"pretty little girl,"* and my mother answers her with a question, *"You think so?"* I dropped my head. Her tone and delivery were playful, but with the heart of a child, I could even feel how unbecoming it was for her to question something like that, notably in front of me. When the lady replied, *"She sure is,"* she smiled at me, lifting my chin as if to say, *"Chin up!"* I knew I wasn't wrong for feeling the way I felt. At that moment, I knew my mother didn't see me as a pretty little girl the way that her parents, my godmother Sonja, and even strangers on the street saw me. What's for damn sure, she didn't treat me that way either.

I remember a woman named Tessie, who she worked with while living in DC. She was an older Jewish woman who always sent me new clothes. I would receive beautiful clothes from high-end department stores like Bloomingdale's and Woodward & Lothrop or Woodies, as they were known in the region. My mother would bring the clothes home to Newport News in big shopping bags, and my eyes would light up, thinking they were gifts from her. Then, she'd make it crystal clear that Tessie had purchased and sent those things to me by her. It could have been easy enough for her to own it. To say she thought enough of me to bring me these beautiful things. Even to deceptively say, "Look what Mommy brought you"—warming my heart and helping me grow closer to her—she refused the opportunity even at a white lie. She did bring them to me. Bring and bought are two words with two different meanings. I wouldn't have known the difference between those two words.

I always felt like everybody *except* my mother was bringing me something. Sonja would bring me coins, or candies, and emotional support. Tessie sent me expensive clothes. I had a cousin named Willie who worked for Krispy Kreme Donuts and would always swing by to see his favorite aunt and uncle, my grandparents, on his way to drop off the local order at the neighborhood Farm Fresh Supermarket. He'd bring donuts for the whole house, some specially picked sprinkled ones for me. My grandmother and Tina always had me ready for the stressful school year, buying me new clothes, shoes, and classroom supplies. Everybody seemed to bring me stuff—extending kindness in small ways, being thoughtful about my happiness, and showing me love in the best ways they could *except* for my mother. Rarely did she express her love towards me, and that shit ate me up inside.

Therapy has helped me understand the differences between my inner and outer child and how they both present themselves in my life now that I'm an adult. I don't usually talk in the third person, so here I go, attempting to explain myself. Whenever I'm working to recover from the feelings of abandonment I first began to experience as a child, and I put myself in that little girl's shoes, I can recognize how my inner child is a feeling being. She profoundly feels things, needs, and wants to be close to her mother. I connect with that part of myself, and I can't help but feel bruised over and over again.

On the other hand, my outer child is a lot more active. When she feels hurt, she acts out. I mean a plum fool. She'll throw a fit trying to put a bandaid on a bullet hole wound. Trying to mend them, hide them, even if she somehow ends up bleeding out, which she usually does. And the grown-ass woman in me wants to coddle the inner child, parent the outer, and figure out how to be the people pleaser between the two and heal.

My therapist, Katie, had me do an exercise where I took an old picture of myself as a child, and my assignment was to tell a story about the image. The story could be about anything I wanted. But all I felt was sorrow and pain when I told my story. With every word that came, I realized how much I hated being warped back into time when I was that little girl because no matter what story I told about her, that little girl's most significant character trait, and perhaps flaw, was the yearning she felt for her mother's love and affection. The saddest part was the older version of myself knew every part, even the ending. I knew what that little girl was seeking from her biological mother was elusive. My mother would never be the woman, mother, or person the little girl needed her to be. So all I could tell were sad stories. Even though I had the most incredible love from my grandparents, my mother's love was what I desired most. Nevertheless, had I come to terms with these truths sooner, I may have been better emotionally equipped to seek, create, and develop loving environments and select healthier relationships compared to the poor choices I later made.

It turns out it *didn't* start with me, after all. The years of dealing with my mother's apathetic behaviors left me feeling empty and confused, unwanted and unloved. I hadn't internalized it until I was old enough to understand that what I represented to my mother was painful for her to accept. If I wanted to be free of the pain her emotions had caused, I had to learn to love her through it without expecting anything in return.

NEVER SAID A WORD

I learned, albeit the hard way, that I would be good without the idea of my mother's love for me. I'd try to insert myself into her life. After a while, I resented myself for trying to insert myself in places that I was not welcomed. In brief moments of happiness or not, I still longed for her. It was for me to think rational thoughts. The internalized rejection created a numbness throughout my entire body. She constantly showed me through her actions that her choice was hers. I wanted her—no, I NEEDED her to tell me who she wanted to be to me so that I could finally feel whole. Unfortunately, she was incapable.

My life was never the same after she moved back to Newport News from Washington, D.C. She was this beautiful woman with warm, glowy skin and a cold presence when it came to her only child. She acted as if we didn't belong under the same roof at the same time, and she quietly shunned me. Not outright ignored but irritated by my presence. I could tell the difference in how she interacted with me and engaged with the man who seemed to be her new love interest. I often caught her in her long flirtatious conversations with this neighbor who lived two streets over on South Avenue, and it was easy to see her mannerisms would change. With me, she was rigid. She hardly talked or smiled. She never tapped my arm when she thought something I said was funny. I barely remember her eyes lighting up when I entered her line of sight. With this man, things were different. She was different.

Occasionally, they'd take me to dinner with them, and I'd witness Al's wining and dining. There was a seafood restaurant in Yorktown called Nick's that he liked to visit. We'd get there, and neither would hardly speak to me much other than to help me determine my order after distributing the menus. I always felt unwanted and out of place in their presence. I could tell I was simply a part of the process. The first time I went with them, I remember only feeling happy about it because I knew I'd get to order the Jumbo Fried Shrimp meal. The more he took us out, the less I cared about the company and the more I looked forward to the food.

FONDA E. WOODARD

Growing up, we had straight Southern homecooked meals—that's the best way I can put it. There wasn't a time when I would come home from school, and my grandmother wouldn't have a fried rabbit or squirrel on the table beside some handpicked vegetables from one of the gardens. Homemade biscuits and fat-back meat swimming in grease with molasses as a condiment always adorned the table as an appetizer. At times, knowing that we didn't eat like everybody else in our neighborhood could be overwhelming. I only wanted to eat canned SpaghettiOs like any other kid on the block for a long time. I was so tired of fried rodents and picking vegetables with my bare hands that I craved sodium-filled cans of artificial colors and flavors. Something as plain as a salad would've been just as lovely. Eating a salad like those who lived across the street, with any dressing on it, would've made me happy any day. So, I took it every time I got to eat out. I'd go out with them to dinner and then be annoyed that I had gone.

Eating at that restaurant with Mama Dessa and Al was draining. Watching them date each other was like watching a boring tennis match before understanding the rules. Everything was a back and forth—one compliment after the other, eyes following each other's every move, hands racing to touch and caress any body part that moved across or underneath the table. I got bone-weary just being there as the third wheel, sitting between them.

Shortly—and I do mean shortly—after one of our few dinners, Al asked my mother to marry him. I'm not sure how long they'd known each other, but I walked past his house to get to school every day without knowing it. I thought I knew most of the neighbors but didn't know him. Hmmm. And I knew just about everybody. She'd only introduced us maybe a few months prior. One day, she asked me hastily, *"Do you think I should marry Al?"* I assumed this was after he'd asked, and she'd already decided. My only thought and question was, *will you marry me?!* I wanted her to say 'I do' to the things I asked, not to some man who just showed up a couple of fried shrimp ago. None of it made sense to me. By this time, I was eight years old and well into the second grade. From where I was standing, it seemed the dial had been accelerated somewhere in the circuitry of her life. I saw in real time how quickly her self-destructive patterns with men could intensify. I couldn't see how much her decision to marry Al while continuing to deny me would impact our lives for the worse.

CHAPTER 4

Darkness Begins

As a child, I used to have foolish dreams of mother-daughter normalcy that troubled me for a while. One of my most remarkable imaginary manifestations was that of me and my mother living happily ever after. Once she moved back from DC, I knew she'd blossom into motherhood. Back then, I was silly enough to believe that somehow, after so many years of being M.I.A., she'd finally turn up and devote even an ounce of her attention to our relationship.

What I imagined was this 'come to Jesus' meeting that she would have with my grandparents where she'd insist on "taking it from here." After having that problematic but necessary heart-to-heart, she'd plunge herself full-throttle into my life—attending parent-teacher conferences, dance recitals, science and book fairs, all with unlimited interest and engagement. You know, the kinds of things most parents, particularly a mom, are supposed to do. I wanted her to do such a great job of reviving her role as my mother that my grandparents would finally have the opportunity to lead their own lives. And she could also realize her capabilities as a parent. My grandparent's days for raising kids would've long been over had it not been for me. As I saw it, they deserved to wave goodbye to me and my mom on the shore while they sailed into the sunset to start a new empty nest journey. Instead of that vision I dreamed of, what I began to awaken to was more of a nightmare.

Some of my darkest childhood days began when my mother married Al after being activated in my life. It was her first executive decision, and I still consider it the worst. After getting to know that man, I was sure she knew and understood that letting him into our lives was a mistake. Before I caught a glimpse of his true colors, I was optimistic, thinking to myself, *give 'em a chance.* So, I started sharing the news about moving from North to South Avenue. Months away from fourth grade, I bragged and told my friends how I would probably move in with my mother and her new husband on South Avenue. I was talking about how I'd beat them to school. Every chance I got, I sounded off about how I'd be closer to Carver Elementary by walking distance. Crossing the canal was a bridge leading directly to the school, which began on the other side of the house next door to Al's. If nothing else, being closer to my favorite place, Carver Elementary, would be the best part about moving out of my childhood home.

  I loved Carver Elementary when I was young. It was undoubtedly considered something special in our house, but many others would say the same across the city. Much like the shipyard, the post office, and the military posts, that school was one of the ties that bound generations of neighboring families together. My mother and her siblings went to Carver when it was George Washington Carver High School. Growing up with my aunt and uncle, they'd leave the house daily and walk to school with band instruments. Watching the morning sunlight bounce off the buckles on the instrument storage cases as they headed down the road, I imagined myself making the same trip as soon as I was old enough. Marching bands were really big back then. To this day, in the South, being in the marching band is as admired as having a starting spot on the football field; in some cities, even more so. My aunt played the clarinet, and my uncle played the snare drum in their blue, gold, and white uniforms for Carver's band, The Carver Trojans. When my aunt won homecoming queen back when she was still in high school, I felt it'd be an honor to follow in her footsteps, carrying on a legacy I was beginning to understand and living closer to those historic grounds made moving in with my mom and Al much more tolerable.

But after the first five weeks into the new school year, my excitement for such a life subsided. Instead of having to gather my belongings and make the significant move to South Avenue, I was told, *"You can visit anytime you want."* Disappointment does not begin to describe what I felt or physically experienced upon hearing that phrase! Hell, visitation wasn't good enough for me. I wanted a permanent placement, just like a foster care kid. My mother and I hadn't spent an entire day alone together since I came out of her womb. By that age, we were long overdue for reconnection, and that only seemed possible if my mom and her new husband were willing to take me in and raise me as their own. The truth was that neither of them was fit for full-time parenting. Getting to know Al as a stepfather and not just some neighbor I'd never met quickly cemented my earlier attitude.

My granddaddy was the man by whom I came to judge all men against. He raised me to not want for anything except the one thing he nor my grandmother could provide, which was their daughter's love. All of the foundations laid could not supplement what I yearned for. My granddaddy loved his family, enjoyed his free time, and took real pride in his position as a civil servant. He and my aunt inspired me to take up a similar profession as a civil servant. When my granddaddy shared his thoughts, he spoke about admirable things, such as work ethic and the importance of giving back to the community. He often told stories of his work—some of his fondest tales were about him ushering in new equipment at the Post Office. He was one of the first employees to be trained to operate the electronic sorting machines as mail sorting transitioned from being done by hand to using new technology.

Whatever the story, it always came with a lesson. My granddaddy didn't just talk for the sake of talking. He didn't say things to people to make himself look better or to hide his true feelings. He sincerely connected with others and helped them genuinely with each interaction. He was real. These days, not very many people are real like he was. He was also very rich in spirit and heart. His dad, William Bennett Richardson (We-yum Bennett), had had several different "crops" of kids with four women, his words, not mine. Mind you, William Bennett outlived each wife.

My granddaddy tells us he was his father's youngest son out of the third crop, and the fourth wife had no kids. As the youngest boy, he still cared for all his siblings as if he was the oldest. My granddaddy did as much as he possibly could with the bit of time and resources he had. It didn't matter to him that some of his half-sisters were old enough to be his mother. He'd keep track of them all and their kids and check in early and often, offering the refuge of housing nieces, nephews, and cousins if he had to. He'd drive to Portsmouth, Norfolk, North Carolina, or wherever the family was to ensure they had what they needed and even some of what they wanted.

I learned the true definition of family and integrity from him. I also learned that he could be swift and unforgiving at times. Even though it pained me to think about what could've happened if things went wrong, I'll never forget when he had to snatch Mr. Jimmie off his feet for talking out the side of his neck about me. It was a kind response that re-established boundaries followed by general neighborly respect. The first thing my daddy did after that whole altercation was give his best friend Bump, Mr. Jimmie's brother, a call to talk about it—Bump, Judy's uncle, was Mr. Jimmie's older blood brother.

"Bump, I gotta come down there to see you, man. Something happened between me and your brother," he told his old friend over the phone. "I need to talk to you, man." When he got to Bump's place, he apologized immediately for snatching his brother across the chain-linked fence. "I just want you to hear it from me, but he said something about my granddaughter that made me mad." From what I know, Uncle Bump accepted his apology on the spot. Still, it never affected their relationship, not one bit, and they never talked about it again to anybody's knowledge. After that, Uncle Bump would still show up first thing in the morning to go fishing on the boat out on James River, but he wouldn't step foot in his brother's yard to say hello. That's the kind of man my granddaddy was, though, the type of guy people trusted, treated like family, and respected his word. That was also the energy he reciprocated. He was always there if you needed him.

Another thing I'll never forget about my granddaddy was how hard he used to work. How there were times he'd come home from doing a 12-hour shift at the Post Office just to turn around and take me fishing before the sun went down or the tide changed. He mastered striking a work-life balance before it was a thing. There was this one time I remember when I was super young when he borrowed money from his sister, Aunt Alvania, who still ran her liquor to make moonshine. She always had cash, lots of it. She helped keep us afloat when we couldn't afford to buy oil to heat the house one winter, and it would mean having to make up the difference in our mortgage payment because we would be short. He offered her the house deed to hold on to as collateral, but she refused. He promised her and us never to be in that spot again. I was a very small girl when he made this promise, but I can attest that it never happened again. He didn't get a second job, start a side hustle, or do anything illegal. He just worked harder at the one job he already had. He'd often worked his 3-11 shift and stayed until five or six in the morning the next day. For weeks, he'd take this type of shift work.

The kind of man that my grandfather was during his lifetime is incomparable to that piece of shit, Al. There was no absolute comparison at all, except for the fact that their gender is male. My grandfather was a man of principle. He was a man of honor and respect–he commanded the respect he received and gave it when warranted. He was a community and spiritual man. Al was the complete opposite and didn't have any of that. Al was a predator, full stop, and calculated in how he used people. I saw how he swooned at my mom. He talked to her to get her one way to fall for his act at each stage of what little courtship, then began to treat her another once she committed. I saw his manipulative modus operandi with everyone he encountered. It was the same playbook for every situation and person in his life. Straight user.

My new stepfather was not as exceptional or deserving of celebration as my grandfather. I never really knew what Al did for a living. Word in the neighborhood, he was a *"big-time"* GS-5 at the Fort Eustis Army Post. It wasn't until I reflected later in life when I started my government career that GS-5 wasn't so *"big time."* To put it into perspective, the federal government has a General Schedule (GS) pay scale for its General Service employees ranging from GS-1 to GS-15, with 10 steps within each grade, ordinarily. GS-5 is generally considered an entry-level position, which means that the man wasn't big-time but had an essential skill set and barely made any real money. He tried to make up for what he couldn't bring in with his day job with his side hustle of installing intercom systems, lights, and speakers throughout small businesses in the area. He wasn't even a skilled electrician.

One of the things I couldn't stand about Al from the beginning was how quickly he became comfortable in his role as my stepfather. First, he insisted that I refer to him as "Daddy Al." I hated that shit! The only man I called 'Daddy' was the one that deserved the title, not that mean-spirited man my mom decided to marry. Al was too overcritical and finicky to be liked. He was disingenuous, being either extremely sweet and friendly in front of people in public while being unbearably surly and ill-tempered in private. He was a very confusing person to deal with for me as a child because there was no middle ground, and you didn't know which one of these motherfuckers was gonna show up from one evening to the next.

After a while, I eventually learned how to navigate Al's mood swings and odd behaviors, but for way too long, I stayed deep in denial about his teaching me in the den of their home on South Avenue, a.k.a. Lion's Den. He was always wanting to "tutor" me in something. Our lessons would take place after school, once he got home from work, but before my mother came home. As a latchkey kid, I'd usually let myself in and start my homework before he'd get home. Then he'd check my homework, my mother would come home, cook dinner, and then I'd "go home" to my grandparents' afterward. He'd often "join" me at the breakfast bar, where I sat on one of the three bar stools at the counter, dividing the kitchen into two adjoining spaces for cooking and countertop dining. Shortly after I'd let myself in one afternoon, Al appeared beside me as I sat in my usual spot, the middle of the three stools, and asked, "What homework are you doing?"

"Math," I answered uneasily. Only moments before, he'd come home early from work, walked into the kitchen, and noticed the dinner my mother had asked me to take out of the freezer to thaw. After examining it for less than 5 seconds, he picked up the still-frozen package and promptly threw it in the trash as if that wasn't what he wanted for dinner. "You're not so good at math," he said behind me, rubbing my arms with both hands.

Unaware of how to escape the tension between us, my shoulders curled forward, and I hung my head. Anxiously, I kept my eyes glued to the words in my textbook. As I sat in the middle bar stool of the three, he leaned over the chair set at the outside of the counter to join me in taking a closer look, leaving me with that all too familiar feeling of being stuck inside the booth at Judy's house on those uncomfortably rainy days. While we reviewed the practice questions, he'd keep his hand behind me, sliding it slowly up and down my spine while watching me work through the problems and explain them. From the top of my shoulders to the small of my back, if I got something right, I'd regret it because he'd pull me into him tight and close, tell me, "That's good," and proceed to rub my sides and touch me on the front of my chest.

The seconds ticked like hours in those moments, and I wondered how long it would be before he'd move and leave me alone. It wasn't until we heard my mother walk through the front door that I realized I could finally relax. On one occasion, she walked through the house to meet us both in the kitchen. He quickly exited through its side door without saying another word. By the time she reached the kitchen where he'd just been with me. Al had already started a conversation with the next-door neighbors, the Taltons, peacefully sitting beneath the tree in their backyard. I was so disgusted I could cry, but the discomfort of the shame made me shrink more into myself.

By the fifth and sixth grades, my body had begun to develop, and Al seemed to want to help me with my studies more and more. His favorite subject to teach turned out to be human anatomy. I never came home with any papers about the body that we needed to discuss, but he felt it was his job to show me what the male and female genitalia looked like in this vast book he kept in the den. He showed me sexual positions in this book that people should and should not do. With this anatomy book, he'd show me the pictures, read the paragraphs, or have me read the paragraphs associated with the pictures, and then somehow make his way to the highly inappropriate comments he felt comfortable saying to me.

"Don't ever let a man put your legs over his shoulders, or that's gon' hurt you and split you in two, and you'll bleed to death." It was baffling to think about why he would talk to me like that. The first time he told me this, my body filled with nervousness and tension. I suddenly reacted with disbelief and shock when he talked to me. Experiencing those feelings in a room that had previously been so benign to me—with its low-seated couch in front of the only television in the house—was very confusing.

On the other hand, Al's body language was much more confident. He stood with his chest out, reciting the words, pacing back and forth across the room with significant, equal strides, positioning his penis to be visibly noticeable through his polyester pants. It seemed to me as likely an attempt to make it easier to listen for my mother's approaching footsteps while grooming. I distinctly remember him waiting to start the conversations until she'd be in the kitchen turning on an appliance, running water, or cooking some meal on that weird electric stove. It was a retractable stove, Frigidaire Flair. You could pull the burners out of the wall like a damn drawer.

As each of his "tutoring" sessions became more and more explicit about what I should or should not let a man do to me sexually, I'd keep my head down, nose in the book, afraid to make eye contact. Yet, despite how uncomfortable I became with Al's presence and advances, I kept going to their house because I desperately wanted to be in my mother's presence just in case she was willing to show me love or affection. I hoped that if I kept visiting regularly and established a routine, my mother would eventually see more of herself in me, deem me worthy of protection, and spend more time with me. I thought that shift in perception might allow her to finally love me enough and leave him, if not for me, for herself. In hindsight, my desperation made me a more available target for Al to take advantage of.

The more my mom ignored us by staying in the kitchen, the more Al kept his hands on me in what I called the Lion's Den, the other side of the wall from the formal dining room. Al would routinely take me to job sites with him under the guise of being his helper. The story he'd tell my mom and grandparents was that he brought me along to help pull speaker wires or use my tiny body to get into tight crawl spaces. Al would take me to a church or a funeral home to fix speakers and mics and install intercom systems. Coincidently, where many predators tend to prey, not pray, is where he did most of his business—and where he would touch me unbothered and unchecked. I remember those places specifically because they both have a distinct smell that is now tied to my memories of being abused. He'd tell me to stand on a ladder to carry up the microphones we were supposed to be hanging, and his hands would be all over my ass as if it was attached like a chair. And though we'd get the work done, it came at a cost. On the way home, he'd tell me to sit in the front seat, never the back. In the front was the long bench-like seat with a middle seat belt that he insisted I use to buckle up. The whole ride was one big groping session I only wish I could forget. One summer, things only became worse.

Al had a sister named Mary Elizabeth, and she had a live-in boyfriend, a man named Plummer, whom Al referred to as his brother-in-law. The two of them stayed in a little town called Ahoskie in North Carolina, where the summer heat bakes those back woods like nobody's business. During that time, Al would pack us into his Gold Buick Electra 225—or "Deuce and a Quarter," as referred to in the Black culture—and quite often, we'd make the Sunday day trip to visit.

I hated visiting those people. Mary Elizabeth was a morbidly obese Black woman who reminded me of Aunt Jemima, the pancake lady. Except Mary Elizabeth didn't have that sort of welcoming aura like Aunt Jemima's pancake glow, and she damn sure didn't smell as sweet as pancakes or syrup either. Mary Elizabeth smelled sour. She had a stench. She never seemed to wash or bathe properly—she just *"rinsed off."* She would visit us for an entire week at a time. I'd never hear the water run long enough for proper hygiene care. To this day, I never knew how she managed to get all that ass squarely on the commode and get up to wipe herself properly. No matter how often she went in and out of the bathroom, she never came out fresher.

Plummer was worse. He reminded me of a Black Homer Simpson—short, pot-bellied, and not the brightest crayon in the box but a colorful character. His smell was just as sour as his common-law wife's but compounded with a scent of motor oil, liquor, and urine. Their two-bedroom shed of a house reeked equally severely, like the stale, hot air mixed with fresh outdoor dirt on inside floors. If you are from the South, you know the familiar scent of hot outdoors. Though it was two bedrooms, one bedroom for the two of them, a bathroom that I'm not entirely sure had running water, as we never visited long enough to use it, and one bedroom Mary Elizabeth turned into a storage room for her canning.

Canning garden vegetables was a well-known talent of hers. Though I'd never eat anything she fixed because I knew her hygiene habits, there wasn't a chance I'd be eating anything from those Mason canned food jars. Supposedly, people from around town loved everything she made, but she was famous for her *Chow Chow*, a classic Southern type of relish that Southern folk like to put over their greens, especially collards. Considering her hygiene, I wanted none of it. She used to can all different-sized Ball and Mason jars and other kinds of glass containers, like old jelly jars, and she kept them in the second bedroom of their house. I remember that bedroom always being anywhere from cool to cold. They had a pot belly stove that kept the heat up in the winter from time to time, but the fire could go for hours and warm the whole house while that room pretty much stayed cool. It lacked insulation, making it easy for them to use it for semi-refrigerated storage. When we visited, Mary Elizabeth and Al regularly walked my mother into the room and helped her pick items for us to take home. I was left behind in the main room with Plummer, where he sat in a wooden chair facing the front door and the cool room to the left. Cracking the door to the cool room almost closed, Al would stand between the main room in the broken doorway of the cool room and watch both ways like a lookout as Mary Elizabeth held up each can for my mom to examine. With her back turned and eyes glued on the colorful array of green pickling, purple beets, and bright red preserves, Plummer would pull me between his legs and shove his hands into my panties.

Again and again, fear and shame would sit on top of my shoulders, and my body would fall into itself, continuing the shrinking that began at my mother and Al's house in Virginia. Every time we visited Ahoskie, I'd watch my mom walk into that canning room, already knowing what would happen. Stuck between Plummer's legs, I might wince and whine, try my best to move away, but that filthy man would squeeze harder. "I'm gonna give you a little sump'n, and you just shush now." That phrase spilling out of the few teeth he had in his head affirmed to me that what he was doing was wrong. Plummer knew it. As Al watched, he knew it. The thing that bothered me the most to recall during therapy was how dirty his hands would be as he rubbed my private parts raw. You would think he was a mechanic just finishing an engine job with the amount of dirt and grease caked beneath his fingernails.

He would start by placing his left hand inside my panties and work his way to my clitoris. With his right hand, he'd rub the back of my buttocks, and I'd use all the strength I had to squeeze my little cheeks together, but he'd be determined to pry them apart. That's when my heart would begin to race. I could feel it jumping up through my chest and out of my throat so strongly that I would brace myself for the moment that it ended up on the floor. In his attempts to relax me, Plummer would raise his right hand to my back to bend me over his left knee, still working the left hand as before. I should have never known that type of sexualized behavior of "getting my feelings." After a slight struggle, he'd finally succeed at sticking his finger into my hiney. Al would stand there with his porn stache, watching in the doorway, entertained as a lookout. His penis was as hard as when we were in the Lion's Den on South Avenue, allowing it all to happen. The first time it happened, he made eye contact with both Plummer and me, and I knew then that I'd been left in the room with him for that reason. Whenever I was made to share a bed with Mary Elizabeth, she'd touch me between the sheets in the middle of the night, trying to cuddle with me with similar abuse. I felt shame. I realized I'd been asked to stay with her at their house during her regular trips to Virginia for the same reason.

When they carried out their abuse, I'd keep my mouth shut and eyes closed as tightly as possible, thinking, *he doesn't care, she doesn't care, nobody cares. And the ones that do care, if I said something, I'd be the only one to blame for causing my family so much grief.* In my mind, I saw the way my granddaddy lost his shit over the neighbor, saying I was too dark to play with his daughter when his white friends were around. I just knew he'd kill Al and go to North Carolina and kill those fools for what they were doing to his only granddaughter. In my mind, my mom knew. I felt she'd only blame me for any fallout. So, I just cried. I'd sit there, let them do what they'd do, hope it would be over soon, and cry again. Sadly enough, this was just the start of my pain. What followed closely behind was a fracturing of my spirit and personality that took decades to put back together again.

CHAPTER 5

The Sound of Silence

Akey term I learned to name later in life through therapy is Intrafamilial Child Sexual Abuse. Described by the National Child Traumatic Stress Network (NCTSN, 2009) as sexual abuse that occurs within the family by a family member, where secrecy surrounds the act. It had never occurred to me that this had been my experience with Al and his siblings. However, the NCTSN concluded that family members don't necessarily need to be blood relatives, just those considered family. It turns out no matter how much I despised those people, marriage, for better or worse, had made us family, which made my life even more complicated and a living hell.

Once Dessa brought Al into our lives, shame began to incubate in the makeup of my early development. I was most confused about my emotions and how my body felt during every abusive interaction. Although he wouldn't penetrate me for long periods, Plummer would manage to work me up into what I later came to know as *my feeling.* Now, in hindsight, I understand that what I was feeling was an orgasm, but the whole time, I sensed I wasn't supposed to know what that even was. Afterward, I'd cry to myself even more over the shame, embarrassment, and humiliation. I was ashamed to admit that the awful thing that was happening to me would physically feel good at times. I did not understand. I was so confused. So much so that after the first experience of *my feelings*, I found myself masturbating to recreate it, conflicted between torment and pleasure the entire time at such an impressionable age. This conflict of emotions slowly built into a chronic cumulative wound that I just could not seem to heal.

At too early of an age, my sexuality was activated, and outside of being numb, I didn't know how or what to feel. Or if I should be feeling anything at all. The cycle would continue when Mary Elizabeth came to stay with us during her visits from Ahoskie. There would be the touches in bed at night, and Al would touch me in the den. Then, we'd take Mary Elizabeth home the following weekend, and Plummer would be waiting. Before I knew it, time would go by, and it'd feel like I was being touched nonstop, around the clock, all week. My skin felt beyond soiled. It felt foreign, as if it no longer belonged to me. Back then, we'd take baths on Saturday, right before church on Sundays. To conserve water, we'd wash up in the sink, doing something like a bird bath between our days of filling the tub, which only made me feel worse. It made no difference, no matter how much I'd wipe away the dirt and scrub my skin in the steaming hot water when possible. Despite what I might've looked or smelled like, in my mind, I was nothing more than a guilty, filthy, dirty little child. No one should have to experience that. The pain of shame ran deep.

According to the NCTSN, abused children are likely to blame themselves for their abuse, and I was no different. I immediately blamed myself for everything happening to me because no one in my life was saying otherwise. In fact, with her blatant obliviousness, Dessa would make it seem like it was okay. Nothing hurt more than the first time Plummer molested me, and he handed me a dollar in her presence afterward. That was when I knew that there was nobody I could truly count on to save me. I stared at the crumpled bill in his hand, the lil' sump'n he'd promised earlier in his attempts to stop me from squirming, and I adamantly refused the gesture. But Dessa, viewing what I'd refused as disrespect, forced me to accept the money with a happy "thank you." Terrified, I obliged. From then on, I never said a word on the subject and didn't open it again until I was much older.

For a long time, I didn't want to tell anyone about what I was going through. Like many children who've been sexually abused, I worried about the ripple effects of disclosing the truth. In my mind, protection for me was already off the table. It would result in one extreme or another, and I couldn't let my pain impact the people I loved.

Many times, my mother would be right on the other side of the door when I was being touched, but that filthy man was never challenged or spoken to. Self-absorbed, she never tried to check on me or keep me with her. There also would be instances when I'd hear her footsteps on the carpet as she quietly approached the den. They'd stop short of the door, and the silence right outside would give me the impression that she'd paused there for a few moments. In my imagination, I painted an image that saw her straining to hear what was going on with Al and me. On at least two occasions, I was sure I could sense her presence, trying to creep in on the conversation to hear or see what was happening. It was like she'd listened to the vile things being said to her daughter by her husband. Still, instead of barging in and confronting Al to curse him out or just hold him accountable, she'd quickly walk back to the kitchen and start running the faucet or turning on appliances. After a while, it almost didn't matter how loud he got because she'd just make more kitchen commotion with the cabinets or something. It was as if she was too afraid to face what was happening outside her supervision. Some of the most heinous crimes were committed right in her presence. She chose to turn a blind eye, deny it, or both. And I mean that in the literal sense—my mother has one glass eye. I can firmly state, with the utmost confidence, that she would've blamed me instead of taking responsibility for what was happening between her husband and me. The situation was indeed 'out of sight, out of my mind' for Dessa, so I never felt I could trust or confide in her about anything. And from the way she tolerated and accepted Al's nasty attitude and the unkempt, stinky smell of his sister and brother-in-law, I couldn't help but assume that she'd blame me for her marriage not working out. I already felt lonely, betrayed, and ashamed. Being hated was not something my fragile, immature conscience could handle. Giving her more reasons to distance herself from me didn't seem like a good plan or idea. I was so desperate for her attention and love that I sacrificed myself just for the chance to love her, even though I felt she didn't love me.

Although I saw my granddaddy as one of my fiercest and most excellent protectors, I didn't want to tell him either. Over the years, I'd witnessed his temper in reaction to much more minor things. Flashes of the incident in the yard with Mr. Jimmie would flare into my memory if I even contemplated coming forward. I figured that revelation would lead to something grave, something I couldn't fathom being responsible for. And yes, even as a child, I felt embarrassed, humiliated, and guilty for *letting it happen,* and I thought it was my responsibility to expose the truth. But I never said a word.

I didn't want to tell my uncle because I'd seen him locked and loaded on a rampage in the past over something he perceived his ex-wife had done, and it was so traumatizing to me. I wasn't about to tell him shit. A charming and handsome ladies' man, he had the dimples and charisma to sweep any woman off her feet, with the personality to win over everyone as a trusted confidant and friend. But my uncle was also unstable. After enlisting in the military and being deployed to Vietnam, he was never the same again. I didn't know what PTSD was at the time, but seeing him march up and down the streets of our neighborhood Rambo-style, ready to kill his wife over what he perceived to be her infidelity, I knew that what he was displaying was far from stable conduct. He just looked crazy. Mad and deranged. My biggest worry was that if I told him or his father, my granddaddy, somebody would lose their life, and my mother's whole world would be blown to pieces. And, I assumed, as a result, mine would be too.

I reasoned that if I told my aunt, our whole family's business would be revealed because she'd take everybody to court. My Aunt Tina was the college-educated one in the family, so I assumed that if there were that kind of problem, she would deal with it with the police and courts. She'd take the litigious route every time. She was so smart and always had her head in a book. I remember her bringing books home from the libraries at Hampton Institute. I knew she would do what was necessary to keep me safe. I didn't want her to be embarrassed or ashamed of me or of anything involving me. At the time, my aunt was the best thing in my life. I couldn't imagine ever letting her down. I thought the legal route meant that our family business would be out for everybody to hear and see in the courts and the streets. I didn't want her to have to go through the same shame that was haunting me. I didn't want my granddaddy to be mad at her for putting our 'family business' into the streets.

I was just a scared little girl simply trying to regain balance. It wasn't long before my emotions overwhelmed me to the point of asking about my biological father. I was about 10 years old and tired of being silent about the abuse. I wondered if the man who'd never been in my life would somehow swoop in to save me if I asked about him. He'd be my bonafide hero. But the first time I questioned Dessa, she wasted no time letting me know that she wasn't going to tell me shit. "And don't mention it anymore," she said. "I don't want no trouble out of Al in this house."

It boiled my blood to hear her defend that piece of shit! Because the only response I could muster was that I was going to find my birth father on my own, and when I did, I was going to have him beat her *and* Al's ass. And now, her blood was boiling. She got so upset that she told me to go home. That's when I knew that the house they shared would never be my home and wasn't meant for me. It was crystal clear that it would never be. So, as she insisted that I leave, I quickly agreed. "Glad to.*"* I didn't want to be around that motherfucker anyway.

FONDA E. WOODARD

Back at my grandparents' house, I began to be an angry child. Neither one of them was one to trifle with, but there's just something about a man's wrath that will put the fear of God in any child's heart. My grandfather was the man who could make you straighten the hell up as soon as he gave you a look. But being so mad at the world, I'd act out against my better judgment. More times than I can remember, I got whooped with a switch, a skinny branch picked from the pecan tree outside because my grandfather caught me talking back to my grandmother. I was also throwing things and stomping around. My attitude had drastically changed within six months, all because of what was happening on South Avenue. I'd only act worse when they'd tell me that Dessa wanted me back at her house. I knew what that meant. It meant Al wanted me back, especially while Mary Elizabeth was visiting.

When I was alone in the bedroom next to my grandparents, I'd sit on the edge of the queen-sized bed, staring at my reflection in the mirror that sat atop the dresser, unable to recognize what I saw. I'd sit there for what felt like hours, but I could barely stomach my reflected image. It suddenly made sense that nobody protected me because I thought nobody loved or liked me. It seemed to be one extreme or another. In my mind, nobody wanted me. I was the black sheep, the ugly duckling, and now the sacrificial lamb. The self-harm talk that I inflicted on myself at such a young age would have detrimental long-term effects into my adult years. During these moments, it would've helped if my inner voice of love and kindness overpowered the weight of my guilt, sadness, and shame, but it never stood a chance. Instead, my voice was swiftly silenced—forced into submission by a debilitating fear.

The struggle between waiting for my mother to see me as worthy of being protected and holding myself back from screaming at the top of my lungs that her husband was harming me in unimaginable ways was slowly eating away at my spirit and breaking me down. It was overwhelming to think I could recognize all wrong in these interactions at my young, tender age, but no adult had the wherewithal to advocate for me. Not one person even asked me if I was okay or if I needed to talk about what was bothering me. All everybody did was critique my attitude. Al and Dessa would go so far as to tell me that my attitude was why I never got anything I wanted, but they failed to realize that they were the very reason that caused me to act out in the ways that I did—the simple rule of cause and effect. There was no accountability on their part as a couple, let alone individually, particularly her as a mother, to say I stand accountable and responsible for this tragedy.

Child development experts document that children are well on their way to becoming who they are between the ages of four and five; by age seven, they know who they are. You are supposed to pour love into your children at those ages. This is how you get the best results from their upbringing. I have learned that you cannot expect a great harvest without sowing great seeds in the right soil. I knew that from my granddaddy. How can parents expect exceptional behavior from children who have parents who demonstrate less than exceptional behavior? You get what you give. The result is Familial Karma Trauma Drama, defined as the family dysfunction of unresolved trauma playing out on the living room floor as a stage across generations, continuously creating an entire cycle of negative experiences with drama and unrest.

While my mother and her predator of a husband never fully understood that concept, they were the antagonists in my family drama. They refused to account for their behavior and make a direct connection—a lack of pouring the good into me at intermittent stages of my life affected mine. Fortunately, my grandparents provided an environment that ingrained within me the power of love and what it meant to be cared for and nurtured correctly, but I couldn't shake this desire to be in my mother's life. And as times go, technology improves. By the mid-70s, technology shifted society, and it was becoming more and more challenging to connect on the same level as we previously had. When we began to have more than one or two radio stations to choose from and more than one or two devices to interact with, my grandparents fell woefully behind. I'd get in trouble for not being able to communicate things correctly when it had never been demonstrated or taught to me.

Communication had never become my strong suit as I lacked in its practice. No one ever sat me aside and talked to me when I acted out as a child. However, as determined as I was about remaining silent, that kind of openness and safe space for me to speak up was what I truly craved. I just wanted someone to ask. I wanted to be shown deep care that allowed me to trust and communicate.

I could not cope with my pain, let alone give a voice to it or the crushing weight of the shame that had ascended upon my mind, body, and spirit. I lacked the mental tools necessary to process any of it, so the lies I began to tell myself flooded out of the depths of my despair. The staggering truth is that I was never alone, though my false understanding kept me trapped in anguish for a long time. In my efforts to heal from the emotional scars of my abuse, I came across a Rape, Abuse & Incest National Network (RAINN) report that states that every nine minutes, child protective services substantiates or finds evidence for a claim of child sexual abuse. It wasn't until I read it back a few times, then aloud, and internalized the conclusion that I saw myself differently. No longer was I a dirty, guilty child, but according to the facts, I was a blameless victim— one number in a disturbingly large pool of countless others. I then became dependent on RAINN for resources to help me cope. Sadly enough, I realized that growing up without this information or resource harmed me more. The unwelcome thoughts playing on repeat in my young mind said things like, *I'm not brave enough to deal with this. Nobody's ever going to protect me. Nobody's ever going to believe me. I was never enough in the first place. I'll always be alone.* Just imagine what effects those kinds of beliefs could have on a growing Black girl with mounting insecurities. If you stick around long enough, I'll tell you.

CHAPTER 6

Redistricting

Throughout my elementary school history, I never had anyone in my family show up to that building for anything other than to pick me up when I was sick. Those times were usually when my grandma would walk a few blocks over to get me from Carver. Things changed when the City of Newport News went through school redistricting during the 1976-77 school year. I'd walked through my neighborhood for six years to Carver. Still, by the seventh grade, the kids who lived around my way were bused to Sedgefield Elementary, approximately one and a half miles from our neighborhood, with students who did the same from the Denbigh/Ft. Eustis area, but for some, it was a little further. Like Carver, Sedgefield had once been an all-Black school. Still, following the desegregation period after the Brown v. Board of Education ruling, the state had to find a way to integrate the schools and make up for the aging population. At that time, both elementary schools became middle schools, and Sedgefield was where I spent my 7th grade year.

In all those years leading up to the change, I had never had one parent—let alone two—attend a parent-teacher conference or meeting on my behalf. My granddaddy didn't go because of his work schedule. My grandma didn't go because she was intimidated by the process and had limited transportation. Even though it was a new school and a completely different process for me, with Sedgefield being in an entirely different neighborhood, I doubted whether I'd see either of them show up. I wasn't sure they'd attend the upcoming combined conference and student talent night to learn about it. I was sure nobody from my family would be there, so you can imagine my surprise when Dessa attempted to show some semblance of support. I might've thought it was genuine until she and Al arrived at my school dressed to the nines and more than happy to pretend this was everyday participation.

I should've known what kind of show was coming my way weeks earlier, especially after seeing the faces they made in reaction to the interesting news I'd come home with.

"Guess what my new homeroom teacher's name is?" I asked excitedly one day while visiting Dessa and Al at their house. "It just so happens to be the same as yours. Spelled the same and everything."

Having grown up in a small town, I knew that at 12 years old, if someone had the same last name as theirs, it likely meant they were connected in some way–at the very least, a distant relative. It was fascinating with a last name as unique as theirs. I remember how I couldn't wait to get home that afternoon to tell them about the improbable coincidence, but immediately after the words left my mouth, I knew something was up. It was apparent I had struck a cord.

First, they looked at each other, then back at me. With a bit of suspicion in Al's voice, he asked, "Do you know her first name?"

"I think her first name is Ruth," I answered innocently. Then they looked at each other again. Eventually, through listening in on their conversations, I realized their odd behavior was because they knew the woman I was talking about. It turns out that my new homeroom teacher was also Al's ex-wife.

Now why that lovely woman decided to keep that piece of shit's last name after splitting from him, I will never know. We never got the time to discuss anything remotely close to the topic, if we ever would. I couldn't tell you how nice of a school teacher she was or was not because I barely got to talk to her that school year. That's because the morning after Al and Dessa learned about Ms.

Ruth being my teacher, I was transferred to a different homeroom class. My mother hadn't even let an entire day go by after finding out the news before she called the Principal's office to request the change. And when my mother showed up with Al and sat front row and center to show her "support," I realized that none of my mother's actions had ever been about me. She didn't care about her only daughter's preparedness to attend a new middle school the following year. Nor did she consider that daughter's thoughts about the parent-teacher meeting and talent show night. She only cared about herself, ensuring she and Al looked good and presented themselves well.

I wasn't the only one who noticed the act she and Al put on that night. Hell, it was like watching a 1970s daytime soap opera when they walked through the double doors of that auditorium. The curtain had been pulled back, and they were on stage when they decided to show up at Sedgefield. Al had on his best 'leisure' suit, as he would say, lookin' like Lou Rawls and my mother looking like a long lost Supreme performing at a holiday party. He favored Lou Rawls so much so that to this day, I cannot hear, *"You'll never find..."* without cringing. Dessa took it a step further and put on her best dress, although I can't tell you what that best dress looked like in great detail because we could not see it beneath the massive fur coat she had on.

And yes, you read that right—a fur.

A damn fur.

At a PTA meeting, no less.

Even back then, I was embarrassed because I'd repeated these things if you're not getting me: 1. PTA—the parent-teacher association has a very general, routine community educational meeting. There was no need to dress fancy. 2. A DAMN FUR—the fanciest thing this woman possessed in her closet, and here she goes choosing to wear it to my school. From beginning to end, it was a performance—a front she and Al were putting on. It was later confirmed that it was a show to make my former homeroom teacher jealous. Truth be told, it only disgusted me that much more to know that the two of them weren't even getting along during this time. They couldn't come together to pour into me the right way, but they found a common goal: joining forces and showing off for a woman who probably could not have cared less about them. It was perplexing. In real time, I could see that they were there for themselves, not for me. It's times like that when my feelings of abandonment and neglect grew deeper and deeper within me. It seemed like nobody had ever considered what was best for me, a vulnerable child caught in the middle of an ugly situation and going through her own set of significant changes.

I hadn't even turned in my first assignments when I signed out my books from another class. Back then, you had to sign out all the books you needed from your homeroom teacher for the year. Therefore, when I switched out of Ms. Ruth's class, I had to sign them back into her before I could sign any out from my new teacher. That meant gathering all my books initially given to me, carrying them to one classroom, turning around, and signing out the same books with my new teacher and for the new teachers' classrooms. It was an unnecessary process that made me wonder what difference it made to stay where I was. His ex hadn't done anything to me. But their theory was that she wanted to give me a bad grade because I was the daughter of her ex-husband's latest wife. So it was all speculation for grades they paid no attention to. They had no proof that my grades were in danger because of our proximity, but it was obvious that they never really cared either.

As I said, the situation had never been about me. They'd never truly wanted what was best for me because they would've been more concerned with my stability and academic progression if they had. I was already going through a rough transition with new bussing and the imminent start of a new middle school. Adding the extra steps of changing homerooms is not a small change and should've been used as a last resort, not a top priority. In reality, academically and socially, I was already hanging on by a thread, truth be told. On my last day at Carver, a teacher, Mr. Felton, said that if I hadn't been about to switch schools as part of the new school system, he would've failed me and made me repeat the sixth grade. The truth was that I had been struggling for some time since Dessa and her new husband re-emerged into my life, but that didn't seem to matter to them. What was always most important was how they projected the narrative they were happy with and how they felt that story would affect them, not me.

It pissed me off that something as small as Al's ex-wife being my homeroom teacher could impact my life so much. The thought that rang loudest in my head was *that women couldn't possibly harass or abuse me more than y'all already are.* I also hated that no one inside the school seemed to care enough to consult my teacher or the guidance counselor about the reason for the transfer. They never asked her what kind of student I was or if I ever talked out of turn in her presence or misbehaved in her class. How was anybody so sure she had plans to carry out excessive discipline when I'd never even raised my hand to answer a single question? Being caught in the middle of all that foolishness was tormenting. I'm glad I only had to put up with it for a couple more years.

By mid-1978, I was partway through my middle school education at Huntington Intermediate School when Al and my mother's relationship was over. In the months leading up to their big blowout, I'd known it wouldn't be long before they split. Not only had they been fighting more and more every day, but I'd also witnessed Al fondling another woman behind Dessa's back. It was right under her nose, inside their house, during one of the many get-togethers they threw. This time, it was during the Hampton Jazz Festival weekend. The festival came to the city every year, and they'd have friends over for a pre-event. Tina would usually come home with her husband, Jim. On any given weekend, they might be cooking out on the grill in the backyard, so it wasn't anything new. But this particular weekend, Al and I both got a surprise when I walked inside the house to use the bathroom, and I caught him with his hands full of Dessa's friend Sandy's breasts.

I could only assume they hadn't heard me when I entered the front door instead of the side door that mostly everybody walked through to get inside the house. It had to be the reason why they only stopped when I came across them in the den—the same den that Al had molested me in so many times before. It was Sandy's turn this time, except she seemed to like it. But as I caught them rubbing against one another, they both looked guilty. With Al's hands rushing to squeeze the span of skin between her breast and her throat, her eyes stayed closed until the very moment both noticed me standing in the doorway seconds later. That's when they stopped. Al backed away, and Sandy quickly began buttoning her shirt.

I walked away without saying a word and returned to the yard to process the images of what I'd just seen. Sandy had been coming to the house for months and was supposed to have been my mother's best friend. They even worked together. However, in the back of my mind, I'd somewhat always suspected her of being the kind of woman who would get down like that. Sandy reminded me of the actress Pam Grier, precisely when she played Foxy Brown in the 70's. Just like Foxy, Sandy was always showing cleavage. All of it. A lot! She'd have her breasts out all the time, and you couldn't miss them. She made sure they were prominently on display wherever she went, even if it was around her best friend's husband. I had always side-eyed her for that. And Al—well, I always knew he was no good, so his role in it hadn't surprised me.

While I sat alone, away from everybody else, so I could continue to collect my thoughts and process what I had just seen, Dessa kept asking what was wrong. All I could do was shake my head in a no-nonsense reply.

"Well, go get you something to eat," she said, breaking my silence. I went and got something to eat. "Fonda, go grab me that spatula," she might've called. I went and grabbed it without letting out a peep. Whatever she told me to do, I did, just to keep my mouth shut and my feet moving. To be honest, I didn't want her to ask me shit else because if she did, I knew I would have told her what I saw, and I was sure that she would never believe me anyway. The most she would do was blame me for meddling in grown folk's business and me for "letting it happen" as if I had a say in how those grown folks conducted themselves. Oh, I know it sounds unbelievable to chastise a child for an adult's behavior—but baby, believe me, she'd find a way. And let me tell you, it would make perfect sense to her. It was a turn of events I grew to expect because that's just the path that many of our conversations would often follow. Later, I learned about projection and how she constantly used it on me.

Besides, Al found a way to tell on himself shortly after that night, so I didn't have to hold onto his secret much longer. Not even a month or two later, he and Dessa were at odds like I'd never seen them before. I remember walking into their house that day after Al had been on a particularly mean streak. It started with his lunch. Dessa would make it memorable every day, and he'd throw it right in the trash can in front of her. Then, after a little while, he extended the same behavior to his dinner. She'd fix his plate, and he'd get up and throw the whole thing in the trash without taking a bite. On the day I remember, I walked in to find Dessa crying at the table, presumably over another lunch he'd thrown away. Sitting there sobbing, she leaned over and used her hands to cover the spot where he'd slapped her clear across the face. The blow had been so hard that it dislodged her glass eye, and she'd had to crawl on the floor in tears trying to retrieve it. Seeing that, I left to get home and tell my grandaddy what had happened.

Running between houses of South and Center, then Center to Swan, I thought about how weak my mother had looked to me when I saw her crawling on that floor. Like me and my aunt and uncle, my mother was raised in a household with the rule that if somebody hits you, you better hit them back. My grandmamma would say, "If he's a man, he won't hit you, but if a male hits you, well, he ain't a real man, so you need to fight unfairly." She'd tell us, "Ain't nothin' wrong with bringin' an unfair fight to an unfair man. If you need to, pick something up and knock the shid out of him. That's what you do."

I'd always learned never to let a male hit me, and there she was—my mother—allowing a man to hit her. She looked weak at that moment because I couldn't help but wonder why she had no fight left. Why didn't she fight the person willing to hit on her? She talked a good game and had a lot of mouth, but Dessa didn't have any fight, and I could not understand that for my life. Watching her crawl on the floor, searching every square inch for her glass eye, she was a shell of herself, was heartbreaking. Looking at her made me understand why she was incapable of loving. Her low self-esteem would not permit such an act. I didn't know whether to feel sorry for her or to be mad at her.

When I made it home, my granddaddy reacted as I thought he would. I'd caught him when he was just starting to lay down to nap before work. As soon as he understood what I was saying, he jumped out of the house and into his blue Ford pickup. He was going to rescue his daughter. With the shotgun sprawled across the seat, his right arm, and the rifle taking up the rest of the seat beside him, it gave a whole new meaning to riding shotgun. He told me to hop in the back of the flatbed. I did immediately. Within seconds, we pulled up with a hard stop at Al's house as he threw all of Dessa's things out onto the lawn. My granddaddy picked up the shotgun and flung it across his left arm with his left hand still holding the steering wheel, resting the barrel in the groove of his elbow, pointing it at the door with his right hand on the trigger.

"Now hop out and get yo Momma's shit and put it in the back of the truck," he told me. I wondered why he'd wanted me to sit in the back of the pickup instead of the cab—he was already thinking ahead. It was so I could jump out, quickly grab my mother's belongings, and throw them onto the flatbed of the truck from the lawn in front of the house. "When you're done, holler for Dessa to come and get her ass in the truck. She's getting in the cab next to me."

Racing to grab blouses and bras all sprawled out across the grass, I ducked out of the way of my grandfather's wrath. All I could think was, *my daddy is gon' shoot this motherfucker.* But instead, he yelled to Al, now standing on the other side of the front door, "Don't bring your ass out here. I just want my daughter and her shit." So we got Dessa and her shit, and we went right back around to North Avenue.

Driving away, my disgust for my mother and what had transpired turned into deep compassion, empathy, and understanding. I didn't recognize this in my feelings toward her. It was foreign to me. I didn't know I had the compassion to understand what she was going through. I began visualizing her and my history with her parallel to her history with men, watching her sit deflated and defeated in the seat next to my granddaddy, her daddy, with his shotgun. The pang of sorrow and despair for her situation welled up in me. I had been so angry in the past that I failed to empathize. I'd always thought she should've left that house long before. The entire incident evoked such complex feelings within me that I went from sympathizing with her weakness to thinking, *well, that's what you get for hiding secrets. This comes back on you when you don't do right by the people who love you, the people you are supposed to protect. It was a complex and perplexing emotional back and forth.* Then it hurt more to think that she literally could not see, sitting right in her face, the family that loved her.

Witnessing my mother's pain, I began to understand the concept of familial karma without knowing it. I felt terrible for what she had to go through in that house that night, but all I could think about were all the times I was left unprotected in that same house, all the time she had left me, and all the love, attention, and information she'd kept from me right up until then. To top it all off was the danger she put herself and me in because she wanted someone to love her, too.

There was a part of me that believed my mother deserved the heartache. I especially felt this way whenever I attempted to engage with her in conversation about my biological father. The man I often wondered about, her first husband Hillary Curry, was my father. I later found out that it was all a lie, although even then, I knew that wasn't right. Things didn't add up. I felt the truth in my spirit, even as a child. Years later, I'd find out that she'd married Hillary after she'd already found out that she was pregnant with me, which he was okay with up until I was born. When my skin wasn't light enough to convincingly pass for their child, Hillary asked for another of his own. They hadn't counted on the strength of my biological father's Black Baltimore genes, overtaking my mother's high yellow skin and turning it into a mocha-brown baby like me.

Dessa told me that she had refused Hillary's ultimatum then, saying that if she couldn't have her child in Detroit living with her, she wouldn't have any of his. I don't believe that statement much simply because I knew Hillary too later in life, and he told me he wanted her to bring me back to Detroit to live with them. However, he was told no for a very different reason.

Hillary was in his last stint of Navy service when he was supposed to marry my mother. He started working for Ford Motor Company in Detroit when he got out. As Hillary told me, they were barely scraping by. He said the real story was that "Mr. Odell wasn't going to allow us to raise you in instability." That's what Hillary told me.

Years later, I would discover that my biological father's name was John Curtis. They called him JC from Baltimore, and he was a rolling stone. Okay, more like a boulder. We know this because I am the second oldest daughter of seven children by six baby mommas. To add another crazy layer to that family dynamic, my oldest biological half-brother was born the same year, month, and day as me. My half-brother's mother and my mother, both from Newport News lived in the same dorm in college at Norfolk State (Little State), Norfolk, VA. As the McClintock effect would have it, women's menstrual cycles will synchronize when they live together. It's suspected that while my mother and my half-brother's mother were living together in this dorm, their menstrual cycles synchronized, leading to them ovulating and becoming pregnant at the same time. In my mind, our biological father was up all night or wee hours in the morning like a dog from floor to floor. One can only conclude this effect took place with us when you have two children born to two different women in two different hospitals on the same day, same month, same year, approximately 23 miles apart. My brother was born in the original Riverside Hospital when it was over by the shipyard, and I was born at Fort Eustis, McDonald's Army Hospital. I am just saying that you cannot make this shit up. It's just nasty.

What I found even more disturbing was what I discovered when I did a family and ancestral DNA search. The information the algorithm pulls tells you about marriages and gives you records of nuptials and divorce. In those records, I did not find one piece of documentation or substantive evidence that showed Dessa had ever been married to Hillary. Even though we share the same last name, there is no record of their relationship being official in that way. I came across her marriage to Al and her previous husband, Dink, but nothing about Hillary, which confused me even more because I was born on a military base. How did they receive those spousal privileges if they were never married? So many times, I've asked my mother to clear up anything she could, but each time, she would shut me up and shut me down. Even to this day, as I hold the records from the Vital Statistics office proving that Hillary Curry had two marriages that did not include hers, she refuses to talk to me about it.

It was during her split with Al that I saw her destructive patterns. The reality of the statement, *I am my mother's child*, became the mirror of a thousand gazes. She always sought solace and wholeness through the men in her life and their relationships, and they did a disservice every time. Little did I know that I would fall into the same lousy pattern of low self-esteem, self-doubt, and self-pity. The same pattern resulted in me choosing one bad relationship after another. Damn, I hated the fact that I was like my mother after all!

CHAPTER 7

An Uncomfortable Period

By the time I reached eighth grade at Huntington Intermediate, I was becoming a young woman on my terms and by my design. My appearance seemed to mark the change—my attention to self-care and my all-around aura. During my formative years, I'd been a tomboy. The best word I can come up with for this style would be the word unkempt. Back at Sedgefield, my outfits would be a little disheveled as I tried to dress for my underdeveloped body. I wore my hair pulled back towards the nape of my neck in one puffy ponytail resembling a small afro or two puffy ponytails slapped to both sides of my head. The goal would be to save time while taming the unruliness of the kinks and my embarrassment of its texture. But when I got a little older, I recognized how naturally beautiful every coil, wave, and curl sitting on top of my head indeed was. After years of being blind to the existence of my beauty, it became something I finally began to acknowledge and embrace. With a strengthened confidence, I returned to the world a fresh butterfly, having gone through a tough metamorphosis bursting out of the cocoon. Wings wide. Colors bold.

It started with my hair. I'd stare in the mirror and slowly contemplate what it looked like and how it could be better styled. Quickly, I noticed how when I groomed it properly, it was less kinky, more manageable, and a beautiful dark brown. During my eighth grade year, I started wearing it with the ends feather-curled all around in a circle shape that framed my face. *Charlie's Angels* was popular then, and the lead actress, Farrah Fawcett, was one of its biggest stars. The hairstyle she wore while playing one of the show's private detectives became iconic. When seeing me in the hall, some of the other students would call me 'Black Farrah Fawcett.'

To compliment my new hairstyles, I also started wearing different lip gloss shades to accentuate my lips. The clothes, shoes, and jewelry I decided to put on did the same. At Huntington, I wanted to be more coordinated with my looks, whereas at Sedgefield, I didn't care whether what I put on my body matched or made sense. I even started to wear more perfume than the kind you get from the Avon catalog. I used to love getting stuff from Avon back then. If you ask anybody about the Avon shopping routine in the '70s and '80s, I guarantee they will agree with me when I say it was an experience. Flipping through the lookbook and talking to the Avon lady became my highlight. When my grandma would offer to buy me something new, I couldn't resist turning the pages straight to the beauty and fragrance sections.

Between the ages of 13 and 14 years old and every bit sassy, it was apparent that I was growing up. After noticing the little shine on my lips from the lip gloss and picking up the scent of my new perfume, my godmother asked me one day what the changes were all about. "Who you gettin' cute for?" She'd asked as we hung out.

"I ain't gettin' cute for nobody," I answered.

"Yes, you are," she quickly replied. "You like boys, don't you?"

"No, I don't even like them."

"Yes, you do," she insisted over and over. "What's his name?"

"I mean, I do like boys," I clarified. "I just don't like nobody in particular."

It was how I'd felt since elementary school. I liked boys and thought they wanted me to, but only because I was athletic. Or at least that is the way I justified their interest in me. I also liked all the schoolyard games like dodgeball, foursquare, and kickball. I played football with the boys in the street and was a good quarterback—I got a strong arm with a good spiral throw to this day. I figured, of course, they liked me. I was one of the only girls they knew who could play as hard as they did, and I could trash-talk with the best of them. But at that age, I had mixed feelings about it. I didn't fully understand what it meant, nor could I articulate why I felt that way.

In the sixth grade, I was just learning what it meant to kiss a boy with pecks on the lips, and that didn't go well enough for me to keep trying or acting on those feelings in a physical way. I didn't know whether my mouth was supposed to be open or closed, whether my tongue was supposed to be in or out, but this one little fella with his cowl neck sweater (they were all the rage back then) took it upon himself to show me the way of the French. Needless to say, I was not impressed. When he kissed me with his mouth open, he drooled enough in mine to let a piece of loose bread float past my lips. Immediately, I ran to tell one of my newest friends at Sedgefield, Quinn T. I called Quinn 'QT' for short in that she was— short. She was also this quiet, shy, pretty brown-skinned girl who was just like me, floating around in search of nothing but open to meeting, seeing, and knowing everything. The popular uptown girls, the ones from Denbigh with the light skin and pretty eyes, didn't make friends and ignored both of us for precisely the same reason. That rejection alone endeared us to one another as friends to the end. I mostly just loved her energy. She was just as disgusted by what had gone down during my very first kissing experience. That one encounter ended up being my last attempt at kissing a little boy for a long while. After that, I mostly stuck to holding hands if I was interested. About a year later, in seventh grade, I distinctly remember being crazy about a little boy named Eric, the hand I held the most during that time.

I liked Eric because he was nice to me. He was a kind-hearted young man who was gentle and sweet, the type that opened doors for young girls of all ages and went out of his way to pick things up off the floor if you dropped them and look you in the eyes as he handed them back to you with confidence. He'd even stop the other little boys in the hall and say to them, "Wait a minute, pick that up for her." On top of that, he was so smart and curious. He was engaged whenever he played a game, even as simple as tic tac toe. I was drawn to his character, even if he wasn't the most attractive guy in the room. As far as I was concerned, we were birds of a feather. For starters, he had a chipped front tooth. He also had this skinny head, and he looked kind of goofy. But that's all guys in elementary school. He walked with a confidence that was hard not to notice. His deep, chocolate-brown skin made me think he might've experienced some of the same things I did, teased for being dark. The more I got to know him, the more I felt a kinship. The popular, light-skinned girls didn't seem attracted to him, so I was happy. No competition. As conventionally pretty as those girls were, he liked me and not them. And although we ended up calling each other girlfriend and boyfriend, we never engaged in inappropriate behavior. Not even kissing. Our relationship was the true essence of innocence. The most we would do was sit closely to one another and intertwine our fingers. Sometimes, holding pinkies was all we needed.

Eric was my first real childhood crush. After the seventh grade, I hadn't liked anybody else that way. So when my godmother eventually asked me if I was letting boys touch me, I told her, "I can't."

"You can't," she said. "Or you won't?"

"Both," I answered. "I don't know. I don't know if I'll ever be ready for that."

It was one conversation my godmother was always trying to draw out. I could tell she knew something had gone on with me, like she was sure somebody had been touching me in ways that they should not have. But she never outright brought up her suspicions. She needed me to volunteer the information to confirm that something had been happening in my life. It didn't matter to me; I still kept my mouth shut. I was well aware of her mandatory reporter status as part of her career in the juvenile justice system. I'd decided that I would never tell her anything before that day. I knew whatever I said would stir up too much trouble.

By the time I was grown, I had told Sonja about Al, and the outcome was just as I had imagined. Except that trouble wasn't in the courts or the streets like the scenes I'd envisioned in my childhood, but more of a silent strain on her relationship with my mother and, by extension, the family. After hearing everything that had gone on when I was younger, in their house and Al's sister's place, she couldn't help but see my mother in a drastically diminished light. At that point, she immediately stopped coming around to our family functions as much. She even stopped bringing her mom, my grand godmother, who we affectionately called 'Mother,' and her daughter, my godsister, Traci, with her when she did spend time. As an adult, I understood the adjustment, but if it had happened when I was at the age where my godmom was hinting at the unthinkable, their absence might've broken me.

During the years when my godmother was becoming my closest confidant, I was also a hormonal teenager, worried about the pressing issues of my appearance, relationships, and schoolwork more than what had happened to me before I turned 10. I had just gotten my menstrual cycle at age 12, and not only was puberty changing my body, but it was also shifting my mind. I wasn't sure of many things outside of the fact that I wanted to keep the dark truth of my past hidden for as long as I saw fit. Finding a sense of belonging with my peers was more important than alienating myself with a news broadcast that said I'd been harmed far beyond our collective comprehension.

NEVER SAID A WORD

In 1978, when I entered Huntington, I quickly realized that, for better or worse, my classmates would be the people with whom I would forge friendships built to last a lifetime, so I took my social life seriously. Fitting in and enjoying the company of those people I called friends became my primary focus. The truth was that by the time I'd gotten to the eighth and ninth grades, robbed of my innocence, I almost felt near empty—just a more polished exterior of myself. If I were a car running on love, trust, and security fuel, I would have gone down at least three-quarters of a tank. To say that I craved connection at that point is a massive understatement. I required it to regain the innocence I'd lost in the fire that was my childhood.

Many people who went to Huntington came from all parts of the city and had different backgrounds. Before I went to Sedgefield, I had already thought that uptown people had means. People from North Newport News to downtown resided within their means. It never dawned on me that they had projects in Denbigh, an uptown neighborhood. I thought everybody there was rich, lived in big houses, and drove nice cars. I assumed those families came from means and lived a particular lifestyle of wealth and isolation. But the children from uptown, the kids that I met at Sedgefield after the rezoning, like Eric, for example, were an eclectic group, every last one of them just plain different from what I knew. Most of the people in my neighborhood belonged to a dual culture and color palette of multi-brown-skinned Black people. There were a lot of light-skinned Black folks that weren't Black as we knew it. These people were of a different culture. That is where school geography and real life began community lessons on diversity and inclusion. This was the time I put the two together. The U.S. territory of Puerto Rico was the American people known as Puerto Ricans. Also, different cultures of families of mixed marriages of Puerto Rican, West Indies, and other island heritage began to live among us in the North Newport News community living in Randolph Apartments, west of our neighborhood. These beautiful people reminded me of the exquisite mixture of shades that resonated within North Newport News. The uptown people had just as many hues because the world was changing. I loved the urbanest of the community so much, from how they walked to how they talked, that when I went into the 8th grade, I wanted to acclimate myself as seamlessly as possible and be more inclusive with all of them. I wanted to be among the beautiful shades of brown.

For some reason, I felt like I fit right in among the beautiful shades of brown; seeing all these different types of people opened my eyes to what could exist beyond North, Center, and South Avenues. My new classmates introduced me to various classes and cultures that stretched far outside the confines of what I could imagine in my neighborhood. My world was broadening with every new interaction, making the few square miles of my neighborhood that I knew grow smaller and smaller, like the back of my hand. It got me thinking maybe everybody isn't precisely what I think they are. When I began settling into Huntington, I started to believe that people could fit into separate molds from the ones I could see set before them. I'm assuming that drew me to many friends during middle school. I'd felt like the ugly duckling for so long, but I started to understand that I didn't have to be that person. With this truth in mind, I blossomed into the beautiful young lady that people began to notice, the first of which was me.

After the seventh grade, my self-confidence shifted dramatically for the better, but belonging became a prominent fixture in my life. When I got to Huntington, I tried out for a new sport they introduced to interested girls called field hockey. When I was younger, I would play football with the boys, but when I got my first period the summer between 7th and 8th grade, my grandfather was like, 'nope.' "You gotta cut all that shit out," he said. "You can't be doing all that running and playing with the boys in the street." His mindset was that I couldn't do certain sports with boys once I started my cycle. It was time for me to get back to more girlish games where there would be less touching and tackling being done by the opposite sex.

Like the slow trickle effect of Civil Rights in southeastern Virginia, that same slow trickle affected Title IX was also involved. Although the Title IX Amendment was established in 1972, change came slowly through the 70's to our communities throughout the decade following its passing. Title IX is the amendment prohibiting sex discrimination in school education programs that receive subsidized federal funding. This amendment is what made it possible for us to play this sport. It paid for the coaching positions, the uniforms, the activity buses, and everything for sports programs in school systems. When the amendment gained traction, it reached every public school in the state; there were sports teams for girls sprouting up in every athletic program. I loved learning about the sport of field hockey. I loved the game with all my heart. For me, it was educating ourselves about the rules and gameplay that I found to be the most intriguing. An entire group joined the team and immediately set the field on fire with our tenacity. We were as fearless as we were green to the sport. We knew no better while other school teams played with mouthpieces and shin guards. We simply showed up with our kilts, tee shirts, and winning attitudes. We were a force to be reckoned with from Huntington straight through high school.

My other sport was cheerleading. We all had a lot to take in those first days of joining. We'd be cheering, "First and ten! Let's do it again!" some of the girls without any clue of what the hell 'first and ten' really meant. Despite the learning curve, our squad was just as athletic as we were loud. And always synchronized—flipping and stomping, keeping perfect time on beats throughout the routine. As co-captains, my best friend Ra and I made sure of it.

I can recall when I realized I had met a best friend for life right after my first cheerleading practice. I'd tried out for the squad like every other girl by making up an original cheer and performing it in front of a panel of about six judges. It was a little nerve-wracking, but I made it, which boosted my confidence through the roof. After tryouts, at our first practice, I was commanding the room intuitively, like the leader I was. Ra was beside me, telling every girl how important it was to have good posture, guiding them on their toes and holding their thighs if they wanted to keep a tight and stable formation. We didn't know Ms. Walker was watching us when we broke into several small groups the day of cheerleading practice because we thought we'd already been through the wringer with tryouts. We also didn't know that we were displaying the leadership skills of co-captains when we began teaching our teammates and settling debates on the best way to achieve a stunt or formation, but that's what our coach, Ms. Walker, confirmed when she handed us the title.

"Ra and Fonda," she called us over. "I'm going to tell you something right now." Ra and I looked at each other, thinking, oh my God, what is going on? What is about to happen? When we looked back at Ms. Walker, she said, "You two better get to know each other well because you two are my new co-captains. I expect you all to lead this cheerleading squad accordingly. Do you understand me, ladies?"

"Yes, ma'am," we answered excitedly, smiling from ear to ear. We high-fived, and she told us to turn around and face the other girls on the squad.

"These two are your new co-captains. They are leaders on this squad. I expect you all to let them lead you," she said. "The mark of a good team is your ability to be led." As she turned and sashayed away, as only Ms. Walker could, I looked at Ra again and knew we would be inseparable from that day forward.

I went home on the activity bus that afternoon happier than ever, not because I had just become captain but because I had been paired with someone I admired. Being selected to be captains together added that little extra spark that made me ecstatic. In hindsight, I had no idea how much that relationship would shape my life or how greatly I would grow to depend on Ra's unconditional love and counsel. We stayed best friends from that day forward without ever falling out of step, almost like we never stopped cheering as captains and the heads of our squad. Ra and I got into every little thing together. She wouldn't let anybody mess with me, and I would let nobody mess with her. We got into a couple of fights with other females, and we almost got suspended. But the truth is Mr. White, and Mr. Baker were scared of Ms. Roberta, so they just took us back to school and made us sit in the cafeteria until the day was over, and we headed home. From that point, we never again got into any school trouble that we got caught doing anyway.

As I grew, so too did my fondness for boys. When I met Dwayne in the 8th grade, I hadn't had a boyfriend until then. Eric was pretty much my first and last friend of that nature. Other boys had caught my eye since then, but none enough to make me like them in the way I liked Eric: simple, sweet, and innocent. But I did like Dwayne. Something about him made me want to be friends in a way that I hadn't wanted with other guys because no one acted interested. He played on the basketball eighth and ninth-grade teams with his friend, Deon, and he and Ra liked one another. These were the sweetest little first-boyfriend stories. We were co-captains of the cheerleading squad, and they were the star basketball players on the eighth-grade team. So, of course, just like any hormonal teenager in rom-coms, this would be like that, right? That's what I was thinking. I could not turn away an opportunity to fit in with friends. I pretended to do what I thought everybody else was doing. But it turns out, none of us was doing anything! I didn't even know what a real-life in-person penis was supposed to even look like, except what Al had shown in the anatomy books and the print in his pants. I had never seen one in the flesh. But one thing is certain, two for sure: I knew it wasn't supposed to look like THAT! I wasn't about to let that thing touch any part of me. I demanded, "Put it away!" I wasn't having sex with him or anybody any time soon. After that, I noticed that he was giving other girls attention. I realized he expressly set his sites on my friend QT. In my opinion, he sought her out to hurt me because he knew she and I were tight. I turned to walk away in utter and complete silence. My feelings were so hurt that there wasn't much I could say, not by her but by him.

I had a complicated mindset around the subject of sex because of what I'd experienced in my childhood. Before I was old enough to start liking boys or getting to know my body, concepts of intimacy and thoughts of sexual intercourse were extremely anxiety-inducing for me. After everything I'd been through, I was determined to make platonic friends. Nevertheless, shortly after the incident with Dwayne, I realized, while sitting in Ms. Eggleston's home economics class, that I also didn't want to make any babies.

I remember being 14 years old and turning around to talk to my classmate, Katherine, who sat behind me. The image that has stayed burned in my brain all this time is her sitting there rubbing her belly, telling me how she would soon be having a baby. I couldn't believe my eyes or think straight for the rest of the day. I mean, I had JUST started my menstrual cycle. And everything, I mean EVERYTHING, I learned about the menstrual cycle, I had JUST learned within the last eight months. I clearly understood that once you start bleeding, you could have babies no matter what your age or whatever information you did or did not have. That was what my grandma told me when I started my cycle, so that was the extent of my knowledge.

The summer between my seventh and eighth-grade years, she sat me down and revealed part of the truth about my body to me. I had been in the yard practicing cheerleading jumps like my friends Veda and Lisa, who lived in the neighborhood. They were both cheerleaders. I wanted to be a cheerleader just like them. So one day, I'm practicing my moves, and I come down on my feet hard to the feeling of a wet, sticky flush of stink between my legs and into my panties. I looked down at my pants, and running down my leg, little by little, was a fresh pool of bright red blood. I immediately ran inside, yelling, "Ma! Ma!"

"Oh Lord, baby! Congratulations," she said as her eyes lit up. She looked down at the mess in my pants. "You just became a woman. Come on in here. Take your pants off, take your panties off, and change; we're going to get you some pads. Here. Use this tissue," she said as I waddled up the toilet paper, standing in the bathroom, unsure of what would happen next.

Once I cleaned up and changed my clothes, we walked to the Revco drugstore, which was not too far from our house. They sold the pads I would be wearing straight through to high school. Inside the box was a belt that took the shape of a T when lying flat. The top part of the t-shape was what you wore around your waist, and the bottom part was two pieces of fabric hanging down as the dividing line between your legs, one in front and the other in the back. This was before they started adding adhesive to the undersides of pads, so at each end of those hanging pieces of fabric was some sort of clip that you would use to hold the pad into place against your body. You would be able to pull the belt and the clips as tight or as loose as you need to first, and then you would put your panties on over top of the whole contraption. It was so uncomfortable. It reminded you of a g-string with clamps. Back then, there weren't any different sizes, wing shapes, or absorbency amounts either. You had one 12-inch piece of gauze you'd be walking around with, starting at the front of your legs and extending straight up your butt that rendered most movement to be unbearably inconvenient. On the days I had my period, I never wanted to do anything more than sit or lie down for a full 24 hours. As much as I loved cheerleading, the last thing on my mind would be jumping up and down, especially if I had to have one of those pads on.

My cycle grew to become the indicator of my insecurities and confusion during those early years of my teens. I wasn't sure what it meant to reach womanhood. *What does she mean, 'Congratulations, baby, you just became a woman'?* When I came into the house bleeding that day, we had a conversation about the fact that getting my cycle meant that I could have babies, but knowing that piece of information didn't make me feel any better. Those words did not reassure me of anything. The proclamation itself rang hollow within me, and reciting it back didn't make the true nature of the transition any easier. I still had to go to school on the days when my entire insides felt like they were slowly oozing down me.

I'd still have to wear the annoying pads with the adjustable belt and the metal clips. Sometimes, I would bleed through to my clothes, though I could hardly wear pants. Even though pants felt more comfortable to wear, the first couple days of my period, I would try to wear a skirt or some kind of loose-fitting dress— anything that would keep people from seeing the print of the pad running up my tail back. Some girls would have the top of the belt hiked up outside their clothes. The reveal of their menstrual belt would especially happen if they wore any pants. I wouldn't be caught dead in that predicament. It was already bad enough that there was an embarrassing smell that lingered. I would wear extra perfume to mask the scent of a girl on her cycle. And it was hard not to feel some way about what I'd read in the Bible about that time of the month for women, how it's *unclean.* That confused me, too. But you dare not ask anyone in the clergy questions about that. ESPECIALLY PASTOR.

My grandparents used to take us to New Grafton Baptist back then, and I remember Reverend Wilson would be just hootin' and hollerin' in his sermons. One of his sermons, mainly, was from Leviticus 1, about women and their *uncleanliness.* That bleeding time was unclean, and that is when I learned the meaning of discernment. I began to misunderstand the word from the pulpit so that I would read the word for myself. To this point, I remained highly sensitive about my body—how it smelled and who was around me. I was highly odor conscious. I knew of other girls in the locker room transitioning into womanhood. I declared I wouldn't wreak havoc on my classmates, thinking they did it to me. It wasn't until ninth grade that I started wearing tampons, but that was uncomfortable, too. That's when they only had the ones that had cardboard inserts. I learned a lot about the phrase, 'beauty is pain,' trying to be discreet about my 'unclean' time. Sometimes, the pain wouldn't even be worth it because you could somehow miss the mark, and then you'd bleed everywhere anyway, like it just wasn't inserted right. And you had only one time to make the mistake of not having 'extra' in your pocketbook. Whether that meant extra pads or tampons, more clothes in your gym bag, or a combination, you only needed one menstrual embarrassment, and it would never happen again.

That time between 12 and 16 was just an uncomfortable period, pun intended. I couldn't stand that "womanhood" was something that I was going to have to get used to, and quickly. That's another reason why I was more hesitant to be around boys. I was already sensitive about the subject of sex. Still, after speaking with Katherine, I had become hyper-aware of what could happen if you were getting down without protecting yourself. I later realized that Katherine had told me she was having sex during her period. We had a conversation about it that I'll never forget. She talked about how much easier it was to do with the extra lubrication from the blood. *Ewww.* I wondered how she could do that. *It's gotta be a bloody mess. Aren't y'all completely messing up the bed? Or the floor? Or the couch, wherever the hell you're doing it?*

In the eighth grade, I wasn't even having sex, and here Katherine was not only having sex, but she was doing it during the worst part of the month. I thought, *I'm barely kissing boys, and here this girl is with a whole baby in her belly, quickly approaching her third trimester.* I was petrified. Looking back, it left me shook in lots of ways. Health class taught us about ovulation and how missed periods could mean you were pregnant. But sitting there with Katherine, all those teachings became real in a split second. Thinking while watching the "Surviving R. Kelly" documentary, I recalled Katherine's teenage pregnancy, and it all came rushing back to me when they mentioned how he'd taken advantage of many young women between the tender ages of 13 and 17.

These little girls, unaware of being groomed, are not only having sex but becoming pregnant by their groomers, thinking it is love. I struggled to wrap my head around the concept at the time. So did the school administrators when a few little Black girls at school popped up pregnant that year. If I would show up in the nurse's office with a fever, headache, or upset stomach, she'd ask me to tell her whether or not I was having sex. I'd later find out that some of those girls who were pregnant were being sexualized and abused by their mother or aunt's live-in-boyfriends or older family members. They took advantage of their accessibility and proximity to them in their homes. Puberty had just christened these young ladies into their womanhood when their futures got stolen.

The little I knew, I still didn't understand the mechanism by which you could have sex and get pregnant. I'd heard about protection through the streets and Planned Parenthood, but I didn't even have the slightest clue that protection meant contraceptives. I was so naïve. The concept of sperm and ejaculation was way above my novice mind. I had this notion that boys had to pee inside of you to get you pregnant. Yes, that's naïve. It didn't matter how it happened, though I just knew after seeing Katherine's situation that I didn't want it to happen to me. I always imagined being a whole different type of mother than the kind my mother was to me. I had an entire set of goals for raising my children, but being an eighth-grade mother was not one of them. I had big plans for my life that weren't always clear, but I knew being a teen mom would never be a part of the equation. I remember running straight to Ra with so much confusion in my head about why all this was taking place in Katherine's life, and we talked about it.

"I can't believe she's having a baby. Can you believe it?" I asked.

"I know," she said with a worried look. "That's sad because she will have the baby for the rest of her life, and we're just in the 8th grade. Hell, we are babies ourselves," she exclaimed. Now, THAT was my watershed moment—the exact turning point that changed how I thought about being sexually active. It was a moment dividing the line in the sand, separating what I thought I knew from reality. But little did I realize the conflict I would feel about 24 months later when I faced a similar circumstance.

Although I was growing more confident and curious about my sexuality around the time I spoke with Katherine, I was scared about letting boys touch me, thinking, *I gotta be careful, or else*. It was a concept that had already been on my mind since I entered Huntington. After all the things that had taken place in my past, I never wanted anybody touching me. For years, I was defensive. If someone put their hand on my shoulder without me first knowing where, why, and how it would land, I would immediately smack it back down to their side, making them wish they never even bothered. There was one time I slapped the taste out of my friend Deon's mouth when he snapped my bra strap. We still talk about it today, how I did a 90-mile-per-hour, 180-degree, Venus and Serena serve of my hand straight to his face in the Huntington Intermediate School hallway. What he didn't realize was that even a touch that he saw as being funny and jokingly innocent was attached to a trauma that I was still fighting my way through. I was so scared that someone was going to touch me inappropriately that I didn't even like sleeping in the same bed with my cousins if they came to visit. If we had to share, I would wrap myself up like a mummy in the sheets and lay as close as possible to the edge of the bed.

My time at Huntington was somewhat magical as I began to grow into a woman, but it was also tricky and awkward because I was always scared I wouldn't fit in while also feeling desperate to do so. As a teenager, I was starting to make foolish decisions left and right. Pretending to do something I wasn't doing, thinking it would make me fit in, namely sex. Ms. Walker was probably one of my first and only teachers who listened. She was the type that knew more than she said, thought more than she spoke, and knew more than anyone realized, especially when it came to her students. You could not underestimate Ms. Walker. She was one of those teachers who seemed to know everything. She'd known that some of the girls on the cheerleading squad were having sex, and she was guiding them on the use of birth control. She was our version of 'pre' Planned Parenthood. Even though I wasn't doing shit, I still wanted to be like the other girls, so I made up a story about what I was doing so I could get access to her in those conversations, too. Eventually, I felt bad enough to tell Ms. Walker the truth. I wasn't doing anything, and I didn't need anything. I had to come clean.

"Girl," she exclaimed. "What do you think you're tellin' me about something I already know? I know who is doing what and to whom around here." Afterward, laughing and rolling her cat-slayed mascara eyes! All I could do was laugh at myself. Ms. Walker was unique. She knew EVERYTHING about everybody, and she was EVERYTHING to everybody! I swore she had a third eye! I thanked God for her. As a hormonal teenager, I began to depend on her for talks about all things dating, sex, and boys. I still had so many unanswered questions at that time in my life. At home, the subject of sex and sexuality were utterly taboo.

I could never EVER talk to my grandparents about no boy, let alone sex. That shit wasn't happening. My grandma would probably be standing beside him, supporting him in er'bit of his decision. They parented my mother, aunt, and uncle with the same attitude and narrative. I could also talk to my godmother, but only about so much. By this time in my life, she had taken a different position with the state on her job, so her visits began to be more infrequent. My mother wouldn't even talk to me about the weather, so the thought of having a conversation with her about what was going on with my body, sex, or boys was laughable. My aunt, who might've been the only other adult I considered talking to during this time, was living in Maryland and working in Washington, D.C. She'd come home intermittently to visit. Still, when she was around, she wasn't probing me for the details of my social life like my godmom. Instead, she'd ask me about school, grades, and classes— nothing in-depth about my experiences with friends, sex, or boys. Nobody was having those crucial conversations with me besides some of my classmate friends, Ms. Walker, and the occasional school nurse questioning your sexual activity. The subject was taboo.

Vulnerability was a complex emotion that quickly defined my childhood, particularly my teenage years, that left me exposed to risks that I didn't even realize. I always knew it wasn't helpful for me to stay silent, but I just had trust issues. My lack of trust in people to protect me and watch out for my best interests faded. I even had difficulty figuring out people's intentions as they approached me and what their words and actions were supposed to mean on the backend. For example, when people would call me 'Black Farrah' because of how I wore my hair, it was hard to decipher whether that was a sincere compliment or a backhanded dig. I would scrutinize everything that way. It was a large part of my insecurities. Trying to decipher if they were being kind or pleasant for the sake of the action or to make fun of me, I didn't always know and was always suspicious. Over the years, I had been so self-conscious about my skin, hair, and every other little thing that made me different that I would mean mug some of the people who just really wanted to extend a kind word or simply be polite. One thing I knew was that kids could be mean. Most were just trying to be friendly, complimenting my style and appearance, and being genuinely friendly.

Every moment in my teenage years was an emotional roller coaster, even the bus ride to and from school. For the second year that I was bused downtown in my ninth grade year, I continued to notice even more how differently many people lived from the way that I believed or was used to seeing. It didn't fall on me lightly just how disillusioned I'd been about socio-economic status, class privilege, and how my family lived compared to others. Especially when we'd ride past the projects or out to the neighborhoods where the houses weren't as nice or as big as ours, I couldn't help but reflect on my situation. If my mom was raising me now as a single parent, I thought we might also live here in the projects. A lot of these kids have single moms. If we lived here, maybe things would be different. If nothing else, perhaps we'd be together. Looking out the window, still facing mommy issues, I felt sad, confused, and a bit stuck. It was a true era of melancholy. In high school, as I matured, or so I thought, things would only worsen. Making some of the worst decisions of my life.

CHAPTER 8

High School Firsts

High school was a season of monumental firsts, like my first serious boyfriend, Shel. Unfortunately, after I lost my virginity to him, he turned out to be my first heartbreak, too. I didn't know then that it happens in most young love cases, and it's almost always that way in high school! On a brighter note, our field hockey team celebrated a regional championship win together in consecutive seasons. The darker spot was in my senior year of high school. I would not cheer since I'd started in middle school. I was too busy and preoccupied with dealing with the fallout of my reputation, the first of three abortions, and the withering of the relationship that had brought it and never should have been. It wasn't until I was shot up with heroin by that teacher love interest I'd dated, who said he loved me, that I recognized just how much my life had spiraled out of control.

When I entered Huntington Intermediate, I quickly realized that my classmates were the people who, good, bad, or indifferent, would be my friends for life! What I didn't know was how complex that would be for me. Especially by the time I got to Warwick High. Meeting even more new people through upperclassmen students, learning new ways of school life, and 'doing the things that high school teenagers do' is challenging. When you're a teenager with a newfound confidence and a false sense of maturity, matters are complicated. The fact that I was also still carrying immense pain from a problematic childhood only made my experience of this time in my life worse. A desperate need for belonging often led me to do and say things to connect with others for reasons and in ways I didn't always understand. Sometimes, I still wonder why I chose to

FONDA E. WOODARD

put myself in certain situations with some of the people who occupied so much of my world. Finding belonging in worthy circles is tricky while operating in desperation and fear. It's become a life of paradox. Some people who did not keep my best interest at heart significantly impacted my life. Yet, I'd continued to engage in relationships with them against my better judgment.

Veda was one of my good friends from high school. She was a senior at Warwick two years ahead of me and lived in my neighborhood on Center Avenue. I started hanging out with her, wanting to do everything she was doing. Veda played field hockey and was a cheerleader and a Rice's Nachman's Community Ambassador. I played field hockey, was a cheerleader, and became a Rice's Nachman Community Ambassador. Rice's Nachman was a retail department store that sponsored a group of girl community volunteers. As young ladies, we volunteered throughout the community and often did service work, creating one-to-one friendships with people with intellectual and developmental disabilities (IDD). If Veda was participating in an activity, I wanted to participate, too. She was my homey, my role model. At the time, Veda was dating Andre, who had a younger brother named Shel. They were popular boys who went to another Newport News High School, Menchville. They were a pretty popular duo. Andre was in a band called "CRANK," and he could hold a note. He also had older siblings, a brother and a sister, who were just as handsome, beautiful, and charming and had graduated before them. The whole family had this aura, an entrepreneurial spirit, and a sense of Southern charm.

For many reasons, Shel was my first love. I was foolish over that young boy, it's true. Although short, I couldn't get enough of his big personality, handsome physique, and smile. Even though he never knew about the trauma I experienced, he had a way of making me forget about my past and just enjoy where I was and smile. No matter how life was going, he seemed to make me smile. There are those moments in high school in your teenage years when you connect with somebody, and you swear you'll be together forever. You start planning the wedding, naming the baby, picking out the house with the white picket fence, the big backyard, and the dawg! That was me. I dreamed all the foolish high school teenage dreams. Those thoughts consumed me and ran laps around my head most days because I wanted to begin a new life, thinking the short-lived experience thus far was horrible.

By the time I lost my virginity to him, I was sure that he loved me. I could tell how much he cared about me by the time and effort he put into making me feel comfortable. On the day it happened, he was slow and measured in his approach, knowing I had never had sexual intercourse. As he dragged his fingers across my body, there was no faking that I was afraid. He knew it but made me feel secure. When it finally happened, I was trembling. In my mind, the thought of losing my virginity would mean rejecting the person, pushing them off of me, and running ass naked into the woods because of all my past trauma. He sensed my fears, leading him to move slowly with me. The most uncomfortable moment of all was the painful sensation of my hymen breaking. It followed after we'd already gotten into a comfortable rhythm. He got so excited that he couldn't help but force his way through. Thankfully, the experience in its entirety was not as tormenting as I'd once imagined. It happened in his parent's detached garage after we'd been playing with the notion of doing it, or not doing it, for some time. He said his parents were away in North Carolina. We stayed in the garage, and though I was worried about getting caught, he said his brother would look out.

Tucked within the walls of that garage, I lost myself to Shel in a sensual way I didn't have the words for yet. He intentionally prepared me to receive him in the hours we spent together. He was gentle and sweet. It wasn't as cold as I had imagined. And though he seemed to follow his interests in the exploration of my body parts, he wasn't manipulative or hurried in the way that he met my reluctant response to his touch. Instead, he took his time kissing my body, slowly whispering his intentions and all the things that I meant to him. Even as he slipped on the condom, he reminded me, "we ain't tryna have no babies." After my scary encounter with Katherine and the image of her pregnant belly propped behind the school desk etched in my mind in the eighth grade, I couldn't agree more. Still a bit murky on the details of contraceptives myself, I silently questioned whether I should be wearing something, too. I didn't know anything about rubbers, and though I had talked to Ms. Walker about protection, I remained confused regarding female contraception other than "the pill." My thought was whether or not there was a female version I needed to slip on to protect us both.

As surprising as the first experiences go, and in light of what I went through with rumors and the traumatic experiences with molestation, I still didn't experience '*my feeling*' as I had known from molestation. As sick as that sounds. That is when I realized sex in a relationship was more about intimacy than the sex act alone. I now know in ways Shel was just as young and inexperienced as I was. He wasn't necessarily aware of how to pleasure me to climax. His goal was to make me as comfortable as possible to receive him and to make the moment intimate. Neither of us was mature enough for our sexual encounter to be simultaneously orgasmic. Boys at that age have a one-track mind. Of course, he didn't ask "how was it?" and I didn't tell him either. Not because I was intentionally withholding information. I didn't know how I was supposed to feel. I ended up asking Veda what the encounter was supposed to be like. I was unsure of the outcome. "Am I supposed to be bleeding?" thinking he has made my cycle come on.

"Oh my God," she exclaimed. "He busted your cherry." I looked at her, confused.

"We didn't have any fruit," I mentioned.

"Girl!" As she gut-busted in laughter. She couldn't hold back her surprise at it all. "That's your hymen. Didn't you learn anything in sex education?" I hadn't. I didn't know I was supposed to be bleeding or in mild pain.

"I'm sore," I said to her. "And he put on a condom."

"Good thing he did," she remarked.

"Well, was I supposed to put something on me?" I asked.

"Like what?" she asked, her face broken in wonder.

"Shit, I don't know. Was I supposed to wear a girl condom? You ain't told me none of this!" I said.

Our conversation went back and forth from downtown to North Newport News. Like all teenage girls, I genuinely felt like we were in love up until he hurt me for the second and last time. Like many young boys his age, Shel liked to play the game of double standards. He'd talk to other girls but didn't like it when I started playing those reindeer games. He'd flirt with other girls at Newport News High School in front of me in social settings. I felt he used the knowledge of my insecurities about my skin color as he flirted with girls who looked like those whom I was most insecure about. Most were beautiful, fair-skinned girls with educated two-parent households and seemingly perfect lives, or so I thought. He acted on the greatest insecurities that I had shared with him. Seeing him make other girls smile and laugh like he usually did with me was heartbreaking, intimidating, embarrassing, and hurtful to the 16-year-old insecure girl. At that time, I didn't know it was also the typical high school shit. It was a couple of girls in particular that Shel was smitten with: one at my high school, who was a gymnast, and the other, an uptown girl with captivating eyes. If it wasn't one girl, it was another; if it wasn't rumors about one person, it was about another. Fed up with it all, I eventually broke up with him. His little friendship ring meant nothing to me. And he knew when I finally threw it at him it was over.

"I'm just done," I said one night after getting out of the car they'd dropped me off in, Shel, Veda, and Andre. "You can't keep disrespecting me like this! I gave myself to you thinking this would be special, but there's nothing special about this." Blah, blah, blah. Next thing you know, the ring was flying toward Shel's head. I rushed out of the car to the house to cry in my bedroom. Bah-ha-ha-ha! The first breakup lasted all of 24 hours. Makeup to break up, that's all we did!

We talked. I felt bad about breaking up with him over what he deemed a misunderstanding, so I gave him a second chance. Within days of reconnecting, he disrespected me again. At that point, I was like, "Boy, bye!" I made up my mind that I was going to hurt him because he hurt me. Admittedly, I knew it wasn't a good strategy then. A guy began pursuing me from Menchville, the same school Shel attended. He had invited me to his house to listen to music—something about the nostalgia of vinyl records I love. I took this young man up on his offer, skipped school, and went to his house. I ensured people saw me leaving the school with this boy and returning for a drop-off. And why should he care? We had broken it off anyway. When he caught wind of our encounter, he played the victim. He confronted me shortly after that, accusing me of cheating. I let his imagination run wild and think what he wanted to think. What's good for the goose is good for the gander, right? Nope, wrong—it seems the rules of engagement are different for girls.

"How could you do that to Shel?!" one of my girlfriends approached me in the parking lot and asked me. She intended to show her anger and disappointment with me after she heard the rumor. "I know the rumor is that you went home with someone from his school."

"I did," I said rather nonchalantly.

"Well, the rumor is that y'all had sex," she exclaimed.

"Okay. And if I did..." I responded.

"If you did, that's just wrong." she clapped back.

"Okay, but you know me. You know I—" As I attempted to explain my position.

"Fonda!" She shouted my name as she stormed off without listening.

Suddenly, I am looking at her like, really, the nerve of you. I thought, *This IS high school. It ain't the rest of our life like a baby! Damn.* I began to get this overwhelming sense of not caring about what she or anyone else thought about me. I had heard my granddaddy say, "I have been called worse by better." And "they talked about Jesus. I don't care what you think or say about me." But in reality, as a 15-year-old girl, I did. I hated how she was supposed to be my friend, but instead of asking me to explain what happened, she immediately assumed everything she heard was true. I was angry with her for some time over that nonsense, but I forgave it all. I got it. She was reacting to what she saw as a disconnection between my actions and the person she thought I was. For her to confront me was fair, but not to hear me out was not. She was supposed to have been my friend and know better of me. That alone set me on fire. It eroded my trust in my peers, where it had already diminished. At that age, who can you trust if you can't trust your friends?

That moment taught me a profound lesson. I learned the power of rumors and the consequences of being complicit in spreading rumors, which made me question my maturity. At that moment, I never wanted to use that tactic again to respond to hurt and disappointment. It was too harmful, and the worst was the self-harm it caused. When Shel began questioning me about what he had heard and seeing the hurt in his eyes, nobody was hurt more than me. Never mind that I had seen those same hurt eyes looking back at me in a mirror when he did those very same things to me. Yet, seemingly, I had more compassion for him than for myself. Suddenly, reality hit me differently. Learning the hard way that girls cannot use the same rules of engagement regarding dating habits and rituals as boys. It was the sad truth of the classic double standard.

To add insult to injury, he started dating someone I knew. That hurt deeply because it was in my face. Abandonment has a way of manipulating emotions. My low self-esteem had me comparing myself to others regarding beauty and social acceptance all my life. The sting of something or someone chosen over me cut deep. It reminded me that something or someone would always be preferred over me. At times, it seemed I had been birthed into that low esteem. The emotional recall is the same leech that attaches itself to other parts of your life, just going along for the ride. The instant searing hot pain of abandonment at most times floated up into my chest like a terrible case of heartburn—a feeling that was but all suppressed. With just a few words, I no longer felt like I was enough. I wasn't good enough, confident enough, or smart enough for anyone, and nearly impossible to move on from the relationship smoothly. So, I went home and cried my eyes out to my grandmother.

While I laid my head on her lap, she said, "Wait a minute, why are you crying? I thought you told me you would break up with that little boy?"

"I was," I said. "I mean, I did," I hesitated. "I mean, I was going to…" All my words were mumbled in a crying fit, jumbled together through endless tears into one unrecognizable answer.

"Girl," she sighed and breathed, making me sit up. "Then why did you let him beat you to the punch?" she asked. "Don't ever let a little boy beat you to the punch when it comes to breaking up! If you know it ain't right, break up and walk away. And don't go back on it. Make it a done deal. Now he thinks he can run yo' mind. There are other little boys out here in this world, girl." The words hit me like a ton of bricks. When I considered them, my grandmother's point made so much sense. If I had kept moving forward after our first breakup, I wouldn't have been sitting there crying over him and feeling like a fool yet again.

"You ain't lost nothing," my grandmother tried to tell me. "You are a pretty little girl and way too smart to cry over some lil' boy. You are mo smarta' than that!" Though she always showed me I was worthy of being loved, and my heart received it, it never got through to my mind. It was that conflicted duplicity, and I didn't understand it. She told me everything I am is good, even if I didn't always feel that way. She said, "It's someone else's loss and the world's gain if they didn't like me." She said I wasn't losing anything if somebody didn't care about me or see me in the same bright light. All that mattered, God did. Still, I was tone-deaf. "If you don't think good about yourself, ain't nobody gon' think good about you." She taught me that I was the first person who should be thinking highly about myself, but it took me decades to master that lesson. The damage to my confidence took place years before. I couldn't seem to shake it.

When I got to Warwick, cheerleading and being a starting forward on the field hockey team were everything to me. The transition had been exciting, and I was getting into the swing of the difficult rigor of classes. The big thing for me was trying extra hard if something didn't come easy to me initially, usually math and science. I often questioned why I'd be the last to understand the lesson. *"Am I just that damn slow?"* I asked myself. Thinking back, I was more intimidated by the process of learning these subjects than anything. Primarily, as a young girl, I was taught that the science, engineering, and mathematics fields were too tricky for a girl like me. Especially if you had no immediate grasp of the subject. Technology wasn't a part of the acronym just yet. I was told, "Girls aren't as sharp in these subjects." Moreover, most teachers did not spend much time with students who didn't get it quickly. They just gave you the material and expected you to fight to figure out the answers and turn it in. Or at least, that was my experience.

Besides sports, I participated in extracurricular activities, like the Spanish club and The Earl, our school newspaper. The Earl was how I ended up reconnecting with QT. We both liked the news. She wrote sports stories, and I wrote school and counselor announcement information. I was a really good copy editor, so much so that I received a summer scholarship to Virginia Commonwealth University (VCU). That was when the school newsrooms were physically cutting and pasting typed set pages and photographs using the light board before sending them off to the printer. It was one of the biggest jobs on the newspaper team. The more I pushed to hone my craft, the more my confidence grew, and the more I forgot about the boy who stole my heart.

I learned a lot between the ages of 13 and 17. I began by pouring myself into athletics. I always thought it was disrespectful for some people to consider cheerleaders as non-athletes. Cheering takes stamina, coordination, and heart. It was one of the most physically demanding sports in competition. Field hockey in our area was a very aggressive and mentally challenging female-dominated sport. Its ruggedness reminds you of an intersection of lacrosse and ice hockey. I fell in love with the game as I learned the rules. Learning time management, moving between classes, and figuring my way around was challenging. The narrative around fitness and exercise helping your mental state is true. I was much more focused and felt more accomplished, and my confidence naturally grew.

By this time, my anxiety about the beginning of the school year had subsided. "We just leave it blank," said other students from single-parent homes. Most kids I had begun friendships with came from single-parent families and were accustomed to leaving those items off the form. That was when I realized I was in good company for not knowing some details about parental information. I instantly felt a sense of community within a community. Some were filling out their grandparents' information papers and cards with ease. It was nice to be free of the anxiety surrounding those issues finally. This had become easier over the years.

I moved on from my first love by telling myself I was too mature for him anyway. By this time, I believed that being raised by older people expedited my maturity. For most of my childhood, I often found myself surrounded by older companies, largely thanks to the lifestyle and influence of my grandparents. I was exposed to much older and wiser elders who'd lived decades more than I'd been alive. They had genuinely lived through some trying times. They shared and retold stories of trauma, challenge, and triumph. I listened intently, and every word moved me like prose. I can say that I gleaned life lessons from their testimonials. The window to life and how they made me see things through their lens allowed me to appreciate their struggle. That access aged me. I began seeing the world with a young heart and an old soul.

The older I became, the more I began to think deeper in ways that didn't always benefit me. My thoughts were more complex than my mind or body could process. I developed a false sense of maturity. Understanding how I should act in social situations, especially those involving adults, became harder. In conversations with my middle school teachers, I'd presented the same false maturity. They often told me, "Wow, girl! You're something else." Not knowing that "something else" is not necessarily a compliment, no more than a southerner saying, "Bless your heart." I would also get, "You are mature for your age," and I'd soak in every word, proudly wearing each like a badge of honor. Naively, I failed to recognize that not everyone meant those words innocently.

It was easy to see my male friends recognize how my body was filling out. But I was slower to catch on when it came to older men looking at me and understanding their motives. I'd converse with the male staff at school and between classes and be respectful. They showed appreciation for how I carried on a conversation with them. I wasn't into some of the antics that my classmates were often up to. Once, I remember hearing music in the hallway from the '60s and '70s that one of the building service workers was playing. I sang every word coming down the hallway as I walked toward him.

"Girl, what do you know about that music?" He yelled, visibly amused by my vocal skills.

"I grew up on that music," I told him with an easy smile. He just busted out laughing.

"You know you are still growing up, right?"

"Yeah, but I was raised on that music. That's all we listen to in our house." He laughed again and called me an old soul.

"Yeah, I heard about you," he added. "You're different from the rest of 'em. You stay true, young lady. You stay true…"

His voice trailed off, and I said thank you, happily walking away after receiving his comment as a compliment. But stealing one last glance at his face, I can remember that man looking at me in a way that I'd never seen him look at me before, one that I was beginning to notice a lot when I passed by some of the boys at school. It got to a point where I sometimes said to myself, *let me keep walking by and not engage with them.* If I did, I might find myself in an uncomfortable conversation.

Sometimes, the older guys, school employees, would stand in a group and call me over to them to talk. They'd call my name and say, come over here for a second. Then they'd ask me about some topic, like whether I knew about the school system changing or what activities I planned to do when I got to high school. I'd sit there and have the conversation with them, thinking nothing of it, but as I'd turn around to walk away, I could hear them going, "Mhmm… mhmm… mhmm…" They'd baited me over to talk just to look at my body as I walked away. I'd roll my eyes and smile to myself a little bit. *Y'all old, decrepit motherfuckers,* was my thought. Although annoyed, I was flattered at the same time. I didn't always notice when this was happening. For example, one of the security guards saw me lick something off my nose during lunch in the cafeteria. A few minutes later, he called me to the table he was sitting at with another guard.

"We saw you a few minutes ago," he said with a smirk. "Touch your tongue to your nose," was his playful demand. "Can you do that?" I told him yes, and I did it right away with no questions asked.

"Good Gawd Almighty," they exclaimed, dropping their heads and shaking them side-to-side in unison. It wasn't until that moment that I realized they had set me up, and it was all sexual.

Back then, I was still green about it. Even after I lost my virginity, I was still practically oblivious to what had taken place. Touching my tongue to my nose was like people who could cross their eyes. Completely clueless and not so mature after all.

***

As a result, I stopped questioning many things that came my way and just accepted them because I believed I had no choice. I figured I'd seen it all, and there was no possibility of more. Young people's exposure to things during their youth shapes their beliefs about themselves and the world. Those beliefs are generally demonstrated through our behaviors, sometimes acting out. Those behaviors can often contradict who we are yet shaped to be, not who we are meant to be in our full potential. Our lives can be deformed in an instant like that. I guess this is why, by the time I turned 16 and was a junior in high school, I felt like I was overdue for the companionship of a boyfriend.

I had a crush on someone at my school for quite some time. I'd receive candies and mums during homecoming season, but he never asked me for a date. No one did. It turns out he was just being nice. Most boys weren't interested in dating me, and no one ever asked. I started to find myself, yet somehow, that rendered me entirely invisible to some of the people I wanted to be seen by the most. I struggled to find somebody to attend the junior ring dance with. I cannot recall how my friend Cliff and I decided to go together. I didn't think anyone in my school or class had been attracted to me, not even for social purposes. But me and Cliff never officially dated. We were good friends. He was cool, and it didn't hurt that he was a handsome student-athlete, and we looked good together.

On the other hand, the "no pressure" date was everything. He made it easy to let go and have a good time. We enjoyed cutting up on the dance floor in the decorated school cafeteria. Amid all the gowns and tux, we took pictures to commemorate the event. I was more like a sister from another mister to him than anything else, and we were there for each other's support. We had a great time at the dance. What Cliff didn't know was how depressed I was and how much I needed a friend that evening.

We didn't have to cheer at that game during the winter break. I ended up going to Fort Eustis to support the team. I sat high in the stands by myself, watching from the home side and looking as fly as ever. Suddenly, a JV basketball player from Ferguson approached me. I knew him because he dated one of my girlfriends, Tracey, who was like a little sister to me. They just happened to have the same last name. I'd gotten to know Chubb through her when they'd dated for a hot 5, 10 minutes. He took a seat on the step as I sat in the first chair in the row. Instantly, I realized that he didn't just come to speak.

"Yo, he wants to give you a ride home," Chubb told me.

"And who is he?" I asked, totally unaware of who he could be referring to. Perhaps he was talking about some student who went to Ferguson with him. He looked back and motioned his head towards my upper left, in the direction of his basketball coach, casually sitting up to the left of me. "Not your coach!?" I replied, answering my own question.

"Yeah," he said. "He's at your school now, too." Until then, I had never seen that man at our school, although I recognized him as the JV Basketball coach at Ferguson. As Chubb handed me some weed, he said, "He got something for you."

"Where'd you get this from?" I asked.

"It's yours," Chubb said.

"That is not what I asked you! Chubb, I don't smoke weed." I replied.

I didn't smoke weed in high school. My thing was Virginia Slims cigarettes, much worse, in hindsight. I was great at rolling joints and blunts, but nope on the smoke. Out of my friends' group, I was the only person who could make that joint look like a cigar, or a regular *white boy* rolled up in no time with minimal effort. Everybody was always handing me weed to roll for them to smoke, but it was strange to be receiving any drugs, let alone weed, from an adult, especially a coach. I didn't even want any adults to see me smoking my cigarettes. Are you kidding me? I would have never let anyone see me rolling. I didn't want word to get back to anybody in my family because I was confident that once they found out, I could get my ass whipped three times over things. And I most certainly didn't want that one thing to be weed, especially.

"I don't smoke weed," I reiterated.

"Well, I'll tell you what," Chubb answered, quickly transferring the small bundle back into the pocket he'd pulled it from. "I'm going to hold on to this and keep it. But I gave it to you. Suppose you need a ride home. He'd be willing to give you one."

Looking back and forth between him and the coach, I quickly told Chubb, "No, I'm good." Chubb shrugged his shoulders and left. I thought that was the end of it. However, half time rolled around, and there Chubb was again sitting over the top of my left shoulder like the green Great Gazoo from the Flintstones, started talking, "Alright, so I didn't tell him about the weed, I just told him I gave it to you. So if he says anything about it, then—"

"Just keep the weed, Chubb," I said, cutting him off mid-sentence. "What is he doing giving you weed anyway? Ain't he your coach?"

"Yeah, yeah, yeah," he answered hurriedly. "But he cool as shit, Fonda. He cool."

"Yeah, but just cause he's cool as shit doesn't mean he should be giving me or you this shit! And anyway, why are you back over here? I already said no to you and him."

"I'm back because he really wants to give you a ride home," he says, then continues, "He really likes you." With that comment, as I turned and we locked eyes across the room, he stared at me like I was a grown woman. I ignored the red flags that I had just spoken to Chubb about. "He's harmless," Chubb chimed in.

"A ride home, huh?" I said after thinking about it for a few seconds.

"Yeah, he just wants to take you home." With much hesitation, I told him, "Ok, alright. But I want to leave early," because the tournament was so lop-sided, they could have used the mercy rule to end the game. I told him that he'd immediately relay the message to his coach. "And Chubb, I ain't tryna be seen leaving here with no motherfucking teacher. So we either leave early or late, and I can't be home late."

"Alright, alright, okay, that's cool. Cool, cool, cool." His response ran together as if he was just as excited about Teko giving me a ride home as Teko was about doing it. "I'll go tell him," he said. "And the weed thing?"

"I reckon you will, and the weed is yours, Chubb." He got up and walked straight down to Teko, who immediately pulled out his keys and walked out the gym doors. By the start of the fourth quarter buzzer, I was heading out, too. Already warming up the car, Teko flashed his headlights, gesturing for me to get in. When I sat beside him, he asked how I was doing.

"Fine," I said. "But I'm confused. Why me?"

"You are fine," mildly stuttering as he replied. "No need to be confused. I just wanted to give you a ride home and get to know you." I was still perplexed about why this grown man would want to get to know me. That's when I realized he knew more about me than I could imagine.

"So you smoke weed?" He asked.

"No, I don't smoke weed," I replied.

"That's good, that's good," he said. "But —ahhh you ahhh you still smoke them nasty cigarettes, though?" he said with a mild stutter. We both laughed.

"Yeah, I smoke nasty cigarettes," I retorted. I picked up smoking because my mother smoked, and it looked sexy and glamorous. I enjoyed the nicotine high I got from it. Although I hated the smell. And I smoked the same brand as my mother, Virginia Slims. At that age, I was in a love/hate relationship with everything she did. I didn't realize in that bad choice moment I was more like her than ever. The self-hatred for the things my mother silently influenced and reminded me of most of her misgivings left me exhausted. I went through a whole change from doing things like my mom to doing everything I could to not be like her. If she ate this, I would eat that. If she liked to wear one thing, I had to wear another. Once you get into high school and start to get a little more socialized, mainly hanging around with the older kids, you start doing things you know you're not supposed to do to feel accepted. And I went through some Virginia Slims. Honey, I *was* Virginia Slim.

"Nasty cigarettes are legal, and they ain't gonna get you in trouble like weed will," I responded to Teko. He started laughing and told me what I had said was true. Understand that one of the first signs of grooming is victim selection. He had observed me and selected me based on my vulnerabilities. From then on, he found a way for us to see and talk to one another. He had full access to a plethora of female targets through the school system. He isolated me. It started with the small things, like giving me rides from school, home, and work. By the second semester of my junior year, I had almost earned all my credits, so I only had to go to school for half the day in my senior year. The other half, I worked at McDonald's. Three days out of the week, we would leave school together, he'd drop me off at work, and go back. He was always going entirely out of his way for me. Perpetrators do that to gain victims' trust, lowering suspicion to gain calculated access by providing thorough attention and support while seemingly being genuine and warm. They also earn their trust by gathering information about the child and getting to know their needs, and Teko knew mine. He made me feel like we were in a caring relationship. And we always kept secrets.

Being in a relationship with him was akin to living in an alternate universe. The faux love faded as quickly as it began. When I look back on this part of my life, it is like a moment in time. But those were precious high school moments you do not get to relive when you make life-altering mistakes. It seemed we were immediately official. He laid claim to me within what seemed like days as he desensitized me in our discussions around sex. He effectively isolated me from my peers, putting the word out on the 'school'vine' and making it known I was his property. Once the word hit the hallways, I was off-limits to any high school guy who might have been interested. He made sure the message that I was his. And he reigned terror on me with intimidation and his approval over who would attend the prom with me. From the beginning, Teko plotted to suppress suspicions about me with school administrators and home life.

I fell into his trap. Once he began to fill my emotional needs, he assumed a more noticeably important role in my life. Teko gave me gifts, like sneakers and varsity jackets from when he worked part-time in this sports shop in Denbigh. He was robbing that place blind, stealing a crazy amount of inventory from that business, a massive shrinkage. He'd flatter me by pandering to emotional neediness. He increased his attention and affection whenever I talked about ending our relationship. We would fight about time, how and where we'd spend together, or talk about breaking up. He cultivated a false sense of love and understanding in a way I had never known. He had me convinced what we shared was real. He would tell me that no one cared about me more than him or the way that anyone else ever could. He seemed to exploit the fragments of my identity, long broken into pieces since childhood, and played a prominent role in the toxic relationship I had with him and what made me so vulnerable to him.

I was pregnant by this man three times in 18 months. And three times in 18 months, I had an abortion. Two of those times, he trafficked me to get an abortion at the Hillcrest Clinic in Norfolk, Virginia. The last time, I took myself without his knowledge. On one occasion, he drove me across countless county and city lines. From the Peninsula to the Tidewater and back through Jamestown and Yorktown, to Williamsburg. Our field hockey team was competing in the regional field hockey finals game. I played in the game, not realizing the danger. Fresh off the abortion table, I played in the Regional Title game at William and Mary, which I only later learned could have proven fatal. I could have hemorrhaged to death on the field that day. After the other abortion, he dropped me off in Farm Fresh/King's parking lot as I walked alone home in shame.

Teko's abusive behavior started to escalate the closer I got to graduating and knowing I would be going off to college. He would act like I owed him something, constantly blaming me for the pregnancies and insisting it was all my fault. I didn't pay for the abortion procedures, but he began to carry a massive chip on his shoulder about money. I took note of his increased drug use and thievery from the Denbigh Sports Shop. I had paid for the abortion after graduation but before college.

Each time I went in for the procedure, only three people were in the room — me, the doctor, and one nurse. Teko was never there. The staff would talk to me first every time, gently asking whether I still wanted to go through with it. After I got settled, the doctor and nurse would ask again: Had I changed my mind? There were the sounds of the suctions and metal clanging as the nurse removed the tool from the table and handed it to the doctor. He then placed the cervical spectrum into my body, making it a literal cold and bitter reality. This was the routine for my first, second, and third abortions. It seemed I had become the clinic's most frequented patient. Before the procedure, there were questions about whether or not you were sure you wanted to proceed with your decision. My answer was always the same: "Yes, I want to go through with the procedure. No, I am not having this baby." All I could think about was Katherine, and the only word that kept running through my mind was, *"Damn!"* After that, the procedure happened. And I do not regret it.

I was numb and disconnected from it all. It felt as though I saw nothing but the color white and heard nothing but white noise. I began to have an out-of-body experience where I stood leaning in the corner, smoking a cigarette, watching myself lie on the table bed. I saw a white doctor, a white nurse, white walls, white lab coats, a white ceiling, a white table with white sheets, a white blanket, and white towels with white metal blinds. The only things not white were the sterilized metal tools, the stainless steel table holding the equipment, and the little Black girl lying on it. Standing outside myself like that, watching my body ripped open by strangers, I hoped my life would end each time. I remember closing my eyes on the table and seeing the light look orange through my eyelids. The light was so bright and blinding. It was like a lightning strike, and in that minute, I hated him. I hated myself. I hated my mom. I hated my biological father. I hated the world. In those moments, I hated myself so much that I wanted to die.

On June 14th, 1982, I gathered to walk across my high school graduation stage. I was pregnant by Teko for the third time. I was done with him. I resolved that I would be content with never seeing his face again. I hated how I had taken so long to build myself up, but by the 12th grade, my reputation had been so bad I lost the trust and respect of the student body to represent them as homecoming queen. I disappointed my family, classmates, and neighborhood in many ways. Four homecoming queens hailed from our little section of North Newport News: my Aunt Tina from Carver and Veda, Lisa, and Tracey from Warwick. I had high hopes to be the next crowned queen. But no one wanted someone with such a sullied reputation to represent them as their homecoming queen. And who could blame them?

By then, my image was as ruined as my body. Teko never used protection like my first experience. He was always raw with me, no protection. He never pulled out like he said he would because he told me how better it was! Scared, knowing how fertile I was, I ran straight to Veda, who was at Old Dominion University then.

"I'm pregnant again! Under no circumstances am I having this baby, either, and it's not happening. I go off to college in the summer," I told her.

"Are you taking birth control? she asked.

"Yes!" I exclaimed, "And I am throwing up daily on those things!"

"Oh, they may not work for you if you are throwin' up. They don't even have time to digest and go through your system," she said. All I could do was cry as she comforted me, told me to stop beating myself up, and said, "Just make better decisions from now on!"

I remember being so naive as to protect him over my health and welfare. I didn't want him to get into trouble if anyone discovered anything about my pregnancies. That is how grooming works. It is mental manipulation at its core, where abusers tend to build a relationship with an emotional connection. I knew nothing of the laws against minors or anything about statutory rape - nothing. I was stuck in abandonment mode and genuinely disgusted with myself. Not only did I feel cast off, but I was also abandoning everything I ever thought I could do or be for myself. I started acting out even more at home. My grandparents became strict with me, requiring me to account for my time outside the house. They put brakes on my social life, restricting my participation in certain activities. There is no doubt in hindsight that they probably knew everything. But at the very least, they could sense that I was growing up too fast.

I was moving away from the little girl hanging out on the boat with granddaddy all day or in the garden until nightfall. By the time I turned 16. I had started talking back even to him, and my granddaddy was the last person I would've ever thought to fix my mouth against. Once, my granddaddy put me down with the Rick Flare Suplex in the front yard for talking out the side of my neck to him. Yet, I still took advantage of our age and generation gap. By now, technology was coming into play, and I knew how to work things to manipulate my grandparents, too. I did what most teenagers would, trying to get over their parents. In retrospect, it was behavior I was ashamed of.

Every aspect of my life was spiraling out of control. With every pregnancy, I was abandoning my Christian values and future dreams and hopes of a family, children, and life. I sacrificed my body for the pleasure of this man. Damn. I began to think for sure I was my mother's child. I never explained my relationship with Teko to anyone other than my girlfriends, least of all my family. We all pretended it wasn't happening. But just because we pretend doesn't make it so. When you're young, all teenagers think you're smarter than your parents. Seldom is that the reality.

It was clear that if we stayed together, I would continue to block my blessings, and I knew for sure I would end up in jail for something that would be life-altering for everybody involved, including families.

After feeling like I missed out on doing the things I loved as a teenager, I was tired of tending to this married man, a teacher. And yes, you read that right—this man was married. I'd confronted him about it, but I found out midway in our relationship. As a sorry answer to my accusation, he presented me with the pictures he kept in his wallet of his wife and young daughter.

"You said that you weren't married," I yelled. "You said you just had a baby by this woman, but you were never married to her!"

"Well, that was true," he started. "But I did end up marrying her." This confession took place *after* he had already established a relationship with me. After he knew that he had groomed me to be in the place I was already in. Once his sexual abuse started to occur, he commonly used secrecy, blame, and threats to keep me in line, participate, and continue the silence. He maintained control through emotional manipulation, making me believe he was the only person who would love me. I felt that the loss of the relationship, or the consequences of exposing it, would be more damaging and humiliating than continuing the relationship, though it was unhealthy. I felt out of control and mad to the point of suicidal thoughts.

I was hot. Still, he kept trying to explain. One of his ways of showing me favor was by taking me to their family home. We did this several times, and he would show me his daughter's bedroom and the one he shared with his wife. His narcissistic behavior had reached a new level. I gravitated to the room where he kept his vinyl album collection and sat with him on the floor, exploring his music. He wanted desperately to have sex with me in his family home. I would not do it. He got so angry with me that I wanted to leave. I went to the bathroom, and as I finished washing my hands, I began to fix my hair. He told me, "You can't leave all that hair on the sink and stuff. Somebody's gonna know." It was confusing to me, and he seemed to be having a bipolar moment. In one instance, he wanted to violate his home not only with my presence but have sex, and the next moment, he was concerned about somebody finding hair.

By then, an evil spirit had gotten a hold of me, and I didn't care. No amount of favor he thought he had shown me by being in his home could convince me he cared about me, his wife, or his only daughter. I left hair everywhere at every opportunity. I acted like a root doctor, dropping hair on the floor, sink, bathtub, and on top of their shared dresser. I even put some of my hair on his wife's nightstand after she'd started calling and questioning me. She had every right to be upset and unreasonable. Those phone calls shed light on their relationship and the lies he'd told us both. Surprise. Surprise.

They had purchased a new car. She called to inquire whether I had ridden in it. I didn't deny it. He gave me a ride home. That was the first night he used his JV Basketball player to approach me. She mentioned they had two cars, but the heat only worked in the new car. I remember getting into the vehicle, filled with what can only be described as new car heat. It seemed to come to the point where I was going back and forth with him over shit. I knew he didn't care about her, me, anything, or anyone but himself. Initially, he never did drugs in front of me. But as our relationship progressed and the times I lay with him in the dirty motels, I witnessed him shoot heroin at least three times. We were in a hotel off Mercury Boulevard; he invited me to a room with Craig. I almost sat on one of their used heroin needles. If it hadn't been for the seam in my jeans blocking, I would've unknowingly gotten stuck with a dirty needle in my upper back thigh. He would invite his drug-addicted friend Craig to the motel room. I witnessed Craig forge money orders from 7-Elevens with a mechanical pencil and sharp ruler. They forged money orders to support their drug habit. Teko would purchase a $10 money order. Craig turned it into a $100 money order. In another instance, Teko shot me up with heroin in the back of my right hand while I was sleeping across the bed. I know as I type these words, and as unsettling as it is, re-reading it to myself aloud takes me aback – the shit was out of control!

"I'm always getting rooms for us. Why can't you get us a room?" he'd say.

"Motherfucker, I'm in high school. What the fuck are you talking about?!" I said to him.

"You work at McDonald's, you-you probably makin' just as much as me." Just as much as me? I am thinking, *this nigga is crazy*. He had gotten so out of control this would be some delusional things he'd say. He exploited me emotionally and psychologically, and my physical body had been so abused. I was so brainwashed that I even tried to get the room, but I stopped myself before I followed through with the transaction, thinking to myself, *"What the fuck are you doing? You gotta stop this madness."* I'd had enough of looking crazy and overextending myself for that fool. The last time his wife called me, I told her, "Let me tell you something," I all but spit the words into the receiver. "You don't have to worry about me fucking with your husband no more. What you need to worry about is your sorry-ass husband fucking with me." Click.

I slammed the phone down and meant every word. I knew if he didn't stop fucking with me, she'd be collecting on a policy. I thought she had better ensure it was paid up because I was exhausted. I was ready to go to jail at that point. Three abortions, mental and physical abuse, and manipulation—it all took a toll on me, and I knew if I didn't get him out of my life, things would go wrong. I was spinning. I had to find a way to get Teko out of my life, or I was going to jail. I knew then I needed to find my way to the altar. Though I had not been a regular church attendant at that point, I knew the word of God, and I was unaligned. My start was ending the relationship by any means necessary, or I wouldn't survive. For me, not surviving wasn't an option.

CHAPTER 9

The Cost of Lost Innocence

How I felt about how my life had gone up to that point can nearly be explained in a note I pinned to my cheerleader uniform after the last year of being on the squad.

"To whoever receives this uniform, wear it with pride and always take good care of your grades—that is why I am not wearing the uniform this year! Go Raiders!"

The days leading up to graduating from Warwick High School in 1982 were among the most difficult, humiliating times of my teenage life. I suffered a legitimate emotional crisis to the point where I wanted to kill myself. The worst was that I couldn't tell if anyone knew or cared. I remember being summoned to the principal's office and getting my answer.

Perched on the edge of my seat in front of Mr. Stacy's desk, I sat quietly in the chair as he launched into his interrogation without offering the slightest greeting or explanation. He only asked me one question, "Were you in the room with Mr. Teko ?" There was no reason for me to lie. "Yes," I replied because I had been in his classroom. He asked nothing else. I was in his classroom, where he insisted on me leaving my belongings to ensure he saw me in school twice a day, once in the morning and once in the afternoon. He had a type of control and agency over me that I cannot explain. I would put my coat and book bag in his room at the beginning of each day and pick it back up after the last bell, like clockwork. So yes, technically, I was in the classroom. I thought, *"EVER-REE BODY GOES TO TEKO'S ROOM."* He was super popular. Everyone wanted his time, and he welcomed the crowd and craved the attention. With only one question as benign as that, I didn't even know what the assertion was or what it meant. But then, he turned to his phone on the desk, hit a button, and spoke firmly into the receiver, "Yes, she said she was in there." In hindsight, I know he was talking to someone at the school board.

As soon as Mr. Stacy hung up the phone, he told me to leave his office without making eye contact or saying another word. As a high school principal with an accusation of a teacher having sexual activity with a female student, you would think his level of interrogation would've been more thorough, concerning, and urgent for the minor. But not once did Mr. Stacy ask me whether I engaged in sexual intercourse in that classroom. Neither did he ask me if I had ever been hurt or taken advantage of by one of his teachers. He never asked me if I needed Newport News social services or child protective services to talk to as part of his accountability and responsibility as a mandatory reporter. He never asked me if I wanted to call my family, nor did he ever call the Newport News Police to report an assault on a minor. NOTHING. For that, Mr. Stacy, may your atheist soul rest eternally in hell. You are forgiven.

A few students approached me, saying, "You got Teko fired!" My thoughts and emotions were all over the place! He told people he was suspended pending investigation when he was terminated. Looking back, his vice has always been underage girls. He couldn't stay away from them. His justification to me: "They're just jealous of you," he claimed as we lay across the motel bed. "They want what you got. They want me." I looked back at him, doubting that, thinking, *What I got is a busted reputation and an abused body.* That's not saying much! By then, I was already developing my exit plan. I felt lost during those times, engulfed with such low self-esteem. *Is this just a part of the makeup of who I am? Why do I have such low self-esteem?* I would often ask myself. This extremely low self-esteem, compounded by abandonment, made being alone an issue. I found myself with a man who fed the feeling of self-loathing and falsely filled the void of self-worth.

While some students praised Mr. Stacy for his coolness, there is no denying that he failed some Warwick High School students and the staff who knew better and worked with him. After that exchange, it was clear that he saw me as expendable if he saw me at all. Most teachers who knew about my situation with Teko at Warwick couldn't or wouldn't risk their careers to advocate for me and what I was going through. Some of the administrators I'd dealt with at Warwick, like Mr. Stacy, had taught at Carver when my mother, aunt, and uncle attended. These teachers spent their entire professional lives as local educators. Their legacies were formed when their parents struggled to put them through HBCUs to have better lives. So, risking their family legacy to help one student they viewed as "fast" or "promiscuous" was too high of a parlay bet. Sacrificing all that hard work and a clean reputation to save one little Black girl didn't make much sense. The cost of my protection had to be tough to argue. Teachers don't make much money as is. I cannot imagine their salary back in the '70s and '80s, and to risk that type of advocacy wasn't an option.

When my mother heard about the rumors, it was as if she were the judge, jury, and executioner. It was my name associated with the scandal and drama with Teko. But she constantly made it about her. Worst of all, I could not separate one rumor from the other. It was true that I was seeing him. It was not true about having sex with him in the school classroom. But one couldn't be convinced any differently. It was automatically assumed that if one thing was true, so was the other. She never asked me who or if I was involved, what happened, when and where it occurred, and more importantly, if I was alright. A responsible parent would want to be concerned for their 16-year-old child's welfare. I got none of that consideration. Nothing. She showed no care. It became about her. She claimed I was trying to embarrass her because the news was all over town at the city hall at her job. She made the injustice that happened to me, who was taken advantage of by a grown man, on her watch, about her. According to Virginia law, statutory rape has two statutes, one involves carnal knowledge (i.e. sexual intercourse) with a minor between 13 and 15 years old, the second statute deals with "someone 18 years of age or older having sex with someone age 15, 16, or 17 years of age, which is a class one misdemeanor and punishable with up to one year in jail and a $2,500.00 fine." No one was charged or fined. No one.

There were times that my mother would be so upset with me, and the rumors about me, that ignoring me became her comfort in the least path of resistance. She was mad when looking at me as if it were her mirror. My mother, at times, hated me for being my biological father, as well as hated me for being her spitting image. It was problematic when she couldn't decide which one she hated most, him or herself. Once, during this time, we argued while she was driving to work at her second job with Avon. I still can't recall why I was in the car with her or how the conversation escalated to the point of a physical altercation, but she was so angry she started punching me with her right hand and steering with the other. My first inclination? *You ain't got but one eye on the road. If I wanted to flip our asses over into this street, all it would take is one snatch of this motherfuckin' steering wheel.* I came close, but deep within, I knew better. Sadly, that wasn't the only instance of her attempts to fight me while operating a moving vehicle. It was like she had a death wish for both of us.

When I started hitting her back with just my left hand, protecting my face with the right, my mom slammed on the brakes so hard my head hit the dashboard. That's when I swung the door open and got out, slamming it behind me after I grabbed the little purse I'd been carrying. Looking around on the street to find my bearings, I noticed that I was within walking distance of Ra's & G's house, so I started in that direction, leaving her behind without another word spoken between us. To my surprise, nobody was home when I got to Ra's. Strange enough, Ms. Roberta seemed always to be home. Getting myself back together, I set out to head back to G's house in Newsome Park. When I knocked on the door, G's mom, Ms. Helen, peeked out the front window. When she saw me, she smiled. She let me in, seeing that I was troubled.

Ms. Helen was always so sweet to me. She would take kids into her house like it was her job, and we all thought of her as the cool mom because she'd let us do our own thing without asking too many questions and loving on us unconditionally. We sat at the kitchen table and talked about what had happened with my mother. When I explained what had transpired, she said compassionately, "Baby, your mama is doing her best. And for your mama, the best she can is to make it." She continued, "If she's working a part-time job, she's just trying to make ends meet, so she's angry about many other things than just you. it's just how it comes out. I am sure she means no harm."

"No harm, Ms. Helen?!" I said with a raised eyebrow. "But she keeps talking about these rumors that are going around about me that aren't true…" Ms. Helen interrupted, "It's not what they call you. It's what you answer to." So, for the record, I know Tyler Perry's character Madea says this in one of his movies, but I promise you the character Madea was not the first one to say it. It was just the first to be on the big screen because that's what Miss Helen told me that day when I was sitting at her kitchen table, fresh off a fight with my mother, with compassion in her heart for my mother and me. She said, "Don't worry about who talks about you. It doesn't even matter if your mama talks about you." She looked into my eyes and told me I was so beautiful I shouldn't care. While that filled me momentarily, all I could think was this woman, who was not my mother, could sit across from me and call me beautiful, and my own mother couldn't see it or say it, which gave me pause. It made me realize how much I valued and appreciated all of my friends' mothers, as surrogates, who had poured into me.

More than anything, I still wanted my mom to be compassionate towards me. I needed to be protected from the world. She seemed to care more about what the world would think of her than her duty as a parent to protect me. I remember the time she and I fought in the middle of my grandparents' house like we were strangers in the street over the fact that she found cigarettes and birth control pills in my bag. Instead of taking a moment as an opportunity to talk to me as her daughter about what was going on, she asked in a demanding tone, "Fonda, why ain't you tell me that you were taking birth control and smoking cigarettes?" I looked at her with my cigarettes and birth control in her hand, wondering why she would expect a thoughtful response from me as a teenager with the history of our relationship to such a question with that tone. She wanted confrontation, so I was willing to oblige.

"Fine! I'm taking birth control, and I'm smoking cigarettes," matching her tone and energy, not knowing what else there was to say. Then I closed the bathroom door, standing directly between us. Almost immediately after the door hit the wood frame, she started banging and beating on it. I opened it up, and she got straight in my face and said that she was tired of me being a smart ass with her. Without a second thought, I replied, "Good, 'cause I'm tired of having to BE a smart-ass to you, and I'm tired of YOU just being YOU!"

I wasn't in a good space with her. I was getting ready to go off to college, and I'd already had two abortions and didn't know I was pregnant, ah-gain. To say I was tired was an understatement. If that were the present day, at this point, I would have no more fucks to give.

She grabbed me, and I caught her, and we went at it in the middle of a hallway no more significant than three feet wide. When we pushed each other against the walls on either side, my granddaddy heard the commotion and came out of his room to break us up. Grabbing my mother's arm, he said, "don't make me put you out of this house again." Those words cut her deep. She whipped around, stormed toward the front door, and just left. I could see she was hurt after hearing those words and perceiving her father, my grandfather, taking my side, but she didn't realize there was no side to take. We both lost that day.

I look back on moments like some of the ones I just described, knowing very well that all we had to do was sit down and talk about what was happening between us. I'm sure if there was a space that allowed us to feel safe and comfortable enough to voice our feelings without judgment or ridicule, then we both could have opened up about most things. Reflections on spending quality time talking or in therapy would have allowed us to understand that there was no escaping what had transpired in the past, only the opportunity to discuss and let go to improve our relationship. Unfortunately, there was none of that. Like most families, our family never sat down and had such conversations. Nobody ever talked about the silent issues affecting everybody or what was going on and causing friction. That's just how it was. Too many family members like me suffered greatly from it. High blood pressure isn't the only silent killer in the house. The things we never say a word about are.

There were so many things I had managed to take for granted while under Teko's manipulation and grooming. Academics were at the top of the list of the things I neglected. I was always an okay student, and I generally did well enough to get by in class even though I knew, in my mind, I was still hella smart. One missing factor that I truly believed could've helped me along was somebody in my corner who could cheer me on, check in with me, and help open my eyes to how I should prioritize my grades would have been instrumental. I needed a constant mentor that would be all up and through my business. While there were always people around telling me how smart I was, no one ever took the time to be a constant steady investor in the ways that I felt I needed from the standpoint of an educational institution.

My grandparents are not blamed for what was going on with me. After all, one generation sat between us, and I struggled with many lessons they'd left behind in elementary school. They didn't know what to do regarding the kind of guidance, intervention, or advocacy necessary for me to succeed as a high school student. The same is true for some of the teachers; not all are to blame, although they could have and should have done more. I felt they were close enough to the situation and could've or should've been protecting me instead of participating in the gossip about the person they thought I was. In my opinion, Black culture had a lot of groupthink regarding specific issues back then. During that time, most Black people living in small towns tended to believe what they heard from their neighbors who got their information from someone who worked in the 'school system', they ain't ones to gossip, but they heard 'she fast.' It had to be true because if you couldn't trust your neighbor, then who could you trust? It's a valid question.

My problem was that there were a lot of people around who seemed to be convinced that I wasn't worthy or I didn't deserve to be looked after, protected, and cared for as a child. Instead, they'd base their opinion on rumors about me, my body, or my relationships. Teachers talked about students and their social lives like it was a soap opera, depending on their integrity. We are seen as equals simply because our bodies were developed when they should have been advocated, protected, and educated. We might have been developing and looking like adults, but we were still children. I felt like I was marked by them and even by some adults in my neighborhood. I was paranoid with the same emotions within the walls of Warwick High School and, I dare say, the city of Newport News. I loved my city but didn't feel that my city loved me back. Lack of care, it seemed I had a big sign hanging above my head, covered in bold lettering, *'KICK ME - DO NOT SAVE ME - I AM NOT WORTHY OF THE LOUDEST ALARMS!'* Nobody realized how broken I was and how desperately I needed help, even though the signs were clear that I needed help everywhere. I learned to mask the pain well. In my mind when I finally realized no one would save me, I asked myself, *Why would they?* I reasoned, *Because no one had ever saved me from those dark feelings. This time would be no different.* No one was going to have crucial conversations with me to understand just how damaged I was. I went sable dark.

Teachers, administrators, and family were remarkable at ignoring blinking red lights. Thinking back, I cried a lot during that time. The shame was heavy. I remember my grandmother, my mom, and my aunt were returning to my grandparent's home from shopping. It was after my first abortion. I was so emotional about the whole situation because I couldn't believe I put myself in that position. Before they could enter the door, I met them crying on the porch steps. I immediately embraced my Aunt Tina. "What's wrong?" she asked. "What's wrong with you now?" my mother asked. Each kept asking, and I continued to cry without saying I was bleeding. Eventually, I mumbled that I was bleeding. They'd assumed it was due to a menstrual problem.

"Ahh, did you mess up your clothes?" I lied and said yes. My aunt hugged me tightly after answering, saying, "It happens to the best of us, baby!" It felt good to be heard and held, even if it was a lie. I looked over her shoulder at my grandmother and mother, knowing that they'd be listening even if I wanted to share something in the safety of my aunt's hug. Telling my mother anything was not an option I was able or willing to exercise. If I had told my mother or anyone that I was suicidal at that time, it wouldn't have been considered an actual or real contemplation. It was seen as attention-seeking. In Christianity, suicide is an abomination, I understand. However, just because it is considered such does not mean it is not what some people want to do because of the sheer pain trauma produces. Two things can be true at the same time. Those thoughts ruminated in my mind. It was an all-out spiritual warfare, and it was days I didn't think I'd survive. I would think about my life and conclude that I wasn't good enough for anybody. Sometimes, I didn't know I had anything or anyone to live for. The thoughts would cloud my mind and become a terrible distraction.

My self-confidence had sunk to an all-time low. My mind was cluttered and closed off, unable to learn new things, and my feet felt cemented with the inability to move. Recurring thoughts about my abuse replayed on a loop in my mind. I spent the better part of my 20s, 30s, and 40s seeking to forgive the teachers I hated for so long for not advocating for me. I held them accountable for allowing some of the worst things in my life to go on right in front of their faces if no one else would. My thoughts raced through my mind. *You see this grown man after me. You know the rumors. You know I am a young Black girl. Some of you know my family circumstances being reared by older grandparents. You know what neighborhood I am from. You know me! IT IS SUPPOSED TO TAKE A VILLAGE! WHAT IS HAPPENING IN MY VILLAGE!* It was a plea for help long after graduation. For a long time, I thought that maybe, just maybe, one of my high school teachers or administrators would read the situation long enough to pull me aside and say, 'Look, Fonda. What is happening to you is not your fault. You can't understand what's going on. There are laws against this type of engagement.' Hindsight had me imagine they would have tried to mentor me, give me something to educate myself, or do anything to help me be a better student, at the very least. Wasn't that in the job description? Taking it one step further when I needed someone to say, 'I am more than responsible for teaching or coaching you. I am also responsible for protecting you from yourself and the predators around you.' But not one of them did.

My grandmother was engaged in my education throughout my developmental years, teaching me to read and write when she could barely do so herself. She always made it a priority to make me practice the lost art of long-hand writing. It was one of the things she made me do when I would be upset and act out. She used it to calm me and re-center me. What she didn't know was that she taught me a coping mechanism in times during which I could not concentrate and focus after trauma and that it would be instrumental in sustaining me for the rest of my life. My fight was against flesh and evil forces for the battle of my soul, even as a child. Handwriting was something that I hated but learned to love. It slowed my racing thoughts and calmed me. I struggled with battling suicidal thoughts, fighting them off with weapons of the world. But I knew 2 Corinthians 10: 4-5 held the line for me to fight with weapons, not of the world, and let me know I had to change weaponry. I had to *"be strong in the Lord, and put on the FULL ARMOR of God, so that when the day of evil comes, I may be able to stand my ground after I have done everything to stand."* *Ephesians 6:10-11.* Prayer changes things.

I wanted to put the whole Teko ordeal behind me to focus on my college years. Yet, I reluctantly met with him. My summer started with pre-college coursework at Hampton Institute. I got the call on the hall phone while getting dressed to hang out with a few friends. It was the summer of June 1982, and I was preparing to go out with my pre-college girlfriends. We had just moved into the dorms and had plans to hang out on the block. "Fonda…I just wanna see you one last time. I want to apologize." Teko's light, stuttering voice spread smoothly across the dorm telephone line, gullible me listening intently. By then, he and I were soon turning another year old, coming up in August. Apologizing to me didn't mean anything then because my body had kept the scores, and my exit plan was on track. Most of the time, it was a pair of earrings or a necklace. It was the tried and true hook, bait, and switch–but I fell for his shit again, as usual. I couldn't help to think, *"Here we fucking go again! Why am I in this vicious cycle?"* I had no answers. The re-traumatizing of internalized emotions revealed subconscious patterns I traced and retraced. If nothing else, I reasoned that I should at least retrieve my jewelry, hear him out, and bounce.

FONDA E. WOODARD

Hampton hadn't been my first choice for college, but the truth is, I never really had one. I wanted to attend the University of Maryland, College Park, near my Aunt Tina. We even toured the campus. I loved it. I loved the energy and feel of it. The University of Miami was a close second, but I didn't have the grades, money, or support system for either. Besides, Hampton was the only place I could convince my grandfather to let me go because my aunt had gone there. I wasn't happy about it, but looking back, I know God saved me from myself with His placement. Maryland and Miami in the '80s were prime drug dealer territory. There was money and drugs everywhere for anybody willing to be in the mix and do anything for it. Knowing me, my false sense of maturity, and my small-town upbringing, I might have been dead by now. The '80s were the line snorting cocaine years for Miami and free-basing smoked crack; its byproduct was the District, Maryland, and Virginia's (DMV) nemeses.

I realized that was a very influential time in my life. God blocked those paths as options for my life because He had a purpose for me. Had I gone to one of those schools, I may have been in the middle of some of the biggest drug scandals during that era for those areas. There's no telling what I might have been doing. Perhaps swinging on somebody's pole between Uncle Luke and Two Live Crew in Miami. Or, had I been accepted at Maryland, the great possibility of me being on campus during the Len Bias era, whose death was associated with the Notorious Drug Kingpin Rayful Edmonds—and the rise of the crack epidemic. Only God knows what I would have gotten myself into without His grace and mercy. Girls in the scene back then were running money, drugs, and trickin' to survive the time. IT WAS NOTHING BUT GOD! He always has better in store for us than we have for ourselves. I was exactly where I was supposed to be despite it all.

The only thing I wished was that I would've known that I was about to get my ass beat so bad that night that Teko called. I should've avoided Teko altogether. But my grandfather always said, "Life will teach you better than I can tell you."

Before heading out, I told my friends I would meet them back on the block. I had already gotten dressed. Teko was waiting for me at the front gate entrance to campus. From there, we drove to Buckroe Beach, where we "talked," and he would return my jewelry item. All was well at first. We sat there for a few minutes, discussing all he'd put me through over the past months before and leading up to graduation from high school. Mind you, it was only four days between graduation and the start of pre-college. It was challenging to think about how much he'd impacted my life in such a short stint. Over the brief period, Teko had targeted me, exploited my vulnerabilities of neediness, isolated me in my social circles, blame-shifted, and roped me into a personal world of emotional and physical abuse.

Self-examination revealed I should never have involved myself with this man. Self-empathy allowed me to acknowledge and validate that I deserved better treatment. When I began to prioritize myself and finally initiate boundaries, I asked myself, *Why are you sitting here again?* Everything I believed about this man helped me decide to leave. I had to actively self-motivate to push through the emotional turmoil of the abortions. "I'm not doing this anymore," I finally told him. "I'm not seeing you anymore. Ever. This is it. You lied to me about being married, and I stayed. You lied about how you care about me, and I stayed. Now, I am sitting in this car with you while you try to explain why I should be with you. I know I shouldn't have come this evening."

After that, I felt his hand on the side of my left temple. Instead, as if to comfort or caress my face and convince me to stay as he did in the past, he shoved my head and pushed it, knocking my head against the passenger side window. When I tried to get out, he ripped my white blouse. I managed to exit the car, and he got right out behind me and stopped me in my tracks by pushing me face-first into the sand. The next thing I knew, he was beating the shit out of me in the middle of empty Buckroe Beach. Little did he know I had just aborted his fetus for the third time the week before. He did not realize I had walked across the graduation stage pregnant weeks before having found my way to Hillcrest before starting college. I paid for this one. After all, I lay there by myself the previous two times anyway.

Avoiding his pleas to get back into the car, I finally gathered myself and walked the three miles back to campus alone. With my lip bleeding and my right eye busted, nearly swollen shut, I walked back to campus into the dorm where my girls were still pre-gaming drinks, carrying on, laughing, and having the time of their lives, and it was like the record skipped when I walked in. They all froze as soon as they saw me standing in the doorway. A polaroid could have captured their stunned faces reacting to the fresh red bruise and blood on my shirt from my lip, where he had slapped the taste out of my mouth less than an hour before. My carefully chosen outfit was ripped and disheveled, with a busted gum and lips three times its size. "We're calling the police." Kim, Iris, and Joy rushed to my side, one of them clutching the receiver of the hall phone tightly, fingers ready to dial the number.

"No, wait," Deborah, my best friend from Menchville, exclaimed, snatching the phone back and stopping them from dialing. "You all don't understand. If you call the police, and her granddaddy comes down here and sees her like this, somebody is going to die tonight. Her granddaddy is that kind of man. Like he has pistols, shotguns, and shit, he ain't afraid to use 'em."

Joy said, "Okay." I agreed with Deborah and begged them, "Please don't call the police. Please don't." Deborah stayed with me for the rest of the night, helping me clean up my face as best as possible, get sand out of my hair, and comfort me as only a BFF can.

After that night, I never dated or saw Teko again. I had gotten my ass beat mercilessly on Buckroe Beach and survived, with an understanding that I had escaped with my life—for a fourth and final time. There were other times I was sure my soul had left my body when we were having sex. He'd forced himself inside of me so hard that he split me from front to back with no regard and laughed about it as if I were some paid sex worker. When I got the courage to look at myself in the mirror, I realized I hit rock bottom. These recollections were among the worst memories of my life, and they haunted me long past high school.

I didn't see much of myself after that incident. I did my best to avoid stepping into the path of any shiny surface or puddles of water for fear of self-reflection. I was ashamed to look at myself because it showed something I never wanted to be. When I brushed my teeth, I looked straight down at the bowl. While fixing my hair, I'd focus entirely on the strands. I couldn't stand the sight of my body, which had been used up so severely over the past two years, staring back at me with all its imperfections, so I got dressed without looking. When I dared to leave Teko, I refocused my vision on myself and life's possibilities. I finally was brave enough to fix my eyes on the young woman in the mirror long enough to ask myself one question out loud: *"Don't you want better for yourself?"* The answer was a resounding *"YES!"*

As I remember trying to figure my life out, even before I broke it off, I had already started to want more for myself, but change was hard. Sexual grooming is a deeply disturbing manipulation that deliberately focuses on the psychological and emotional connections of its victims by pedophiles. I was ready, willing, and able to work on my internal conflicts. I needed to change how I saw myself, which worked against me for years. I constantly felt internal torment because of this "pedo" thief. I emotionally spiraled when I thought back on what was stolen in my high school years, my body and all that led me to that night on the beach.

FONDA E. WOODARD

A 1991 Daily Press news article described an undercover sting operation that ended in Teko's arrest for drug distribution but was thrown out of court because he said he used but not distributed. And because he was a JV Coach, he was given the benefit of the doubt. Never mind, the distribution charges were valid, accurate, and warranted because he distributed weed to Chubb and me when he initially approached me. Chubb was one of his JV student-athletes whom Teko coached. Chubb was just as much a victim as I was. He abused his position of trust too. That was distributed to minors. Period. The 1991 article reveals that he was fired from the school system in 1982. However, the reporter fails to state or conveniently leaves out the details about why he was fired!

Little did I know I was the subject of the accusation. This was when Mr. Stacy asked about my presence, and I answered in the affirmative, "Yes." With that said, I vividly remember his arrest and I remember his release because we joined each other shortly afterward and discussed the unfolding drama while lying in a shady motel off Jefferson Avenue, now demolished. The very day, he protested his innocence while taking mine. I found out then, as I had always suspected, that no matter how many lies he had told me about me being "the only one, besides his wife, of course," there were other victims like me. They think their advantage was remaining as silent as I did. All we did was give him cover and enable him to offend and re-offend. Nothing was alleged about the incident; it was true, but he had a cast of enablers throughout the community. His circle of dudes, "his boys," were his enablers. I was his enabler, too.

The Daily Press article further states, "… he spent the rest of the decade with a monkey on his back" when discussing drugs and recovery about Teko. Except it wasn't just the drugs that put a monkey on Teko's back for the remainder of the '80s decade, as alluded to in the newspaper. It was more like a gorilla holding onto his shoulders, made up of the weight of the abuse of young girls, abuse of trust with some of the boys he coached, the destructive path he forged in our lives, and the inability to publicly atone as he did with the drugs. This was my lived experience. I suffered at his hands as a young girl, and there were other girls just like me—and young boys like Chubb whose trust was abused. The girls were as much an addiction for him as the drugs. The boy's trust was violated as their coach. And he abused all three: the drugs, the girls, and the boys.

The news article went on to say that they found evidence of him having sex in a classroom with a Black female student. I assumed that the school system had reached its limit. They were just as liable as far as I am concerned. Had there been a thorough investigation, I, as the accused, would have sat for an interview at the very least. Whether he had sex in the classroom or not remains a matter of question. What I do know for sure is that the alleged Black female student was not me. I never had sex on school property. Had the administration bothered to check my schedule and speak with my teachers, they would know I could not have been in two places simultaneously. I was in class when they suspected the numerous allegations to have taken place with me. Unfortunately, that truth didn't stop the rumors from swirling because most people were already aware of our relationship. When the allegations began, it spread like wildfire. I put myself in this position because I did not make good decisions. I wanted to be genuinely loved and cared for, only to be manipulated and used. I take self-accountability for the position I put myself in, though I was a minor.

CHAPTER 10

Abuse Knows No Boundaries

Dating an older man who turned out to be a groomer was a life-altering experience. At first, it felt flattering—being chosen by someone more handsome and mature, someone who seemed to see potential in me that others seemed to overlook. What unfolded was a slow erosion of all kinds of boundaries. I was sixteen going on thirty, or at least that's what I felt like, and he made me feel his equal. He was older—old enough to know better, old enough to stay away. But he didn't. He told me I was mature for my age, different from the others. I believed him because he was older, and he should and would know. I craved the validation. I thought I was special, chosen. Teko didn't just want my companionship; he wanted my time, my body, my life, my agency, and complete control over me. He would praise my maturity while subtly isolating me, making me believe I was special for being with someone his age and position as a coach in the school system. Over time, I realized that what I mistook for love was manipulation wrapped in attention, abuse, and pseudo-affection. What I didn't realize at the time was that I was being groomed.

He fed me compliments the way someone feeds stray animals—just enough to keep me coming back, but never enough to make me feel full. He called it love, and I thought it was love. But really, it was control disguised as affection, manipulation wrapped in attention. The warning signs were there. That's the cruelest part of grooming: it is a ruse for you to believe you're in control of your own decisions until you're too far in, or gone, to realize you never were in control of anything. The secrecy. The discouragement from spending time with people my own age. The things he said and the way he said them.

He'd say, "You don't need your friends knowing everything." But the biggest red flag? No one stopped it. No one even blinked.

All these lessons came to me slowly: one, age does not equal wisdom; two: not all attention is rooted in respect; and three: silence from those who are supposed to protect you can feel like betrayal.

As slowly as those lessons were learned, it was even slower that I learned to rebuild trust in myself after someone older had taught me to doubt my natural instincts. Most of all, I learned that love without safety is not love. The most painful part wasn't just the relationship—it was looking around and realizing I had not one adult I could trust that would help me make sense of none of it.

My mother, either initially unaware or later unwilling to confront the discomfort, offered no guidance. That absence left a wound deeper than the relationship itself. What I realized is that I also mistook my craving for attention when it was truly a craving for protection. I was craving for structure. For anyone with a voice to say, "That's not okay," or "You deserve better." Instead, I was left to navigate adult consequences with a teenage heart.

When it comes to my mother, I don't speak with bitterness anymore—I say it with the ache of a wound I didn't have the words to articulate back then. I needed her. I needed her to see me, to *see* what was happening to her only child, for her to care enough to act and do what's right. But she didn't. Perhaps, she didn't know what to say. Perhaps, she didn't know how to say it, whatever 'it' was. Perhaps she was frozen in time, rendered deaf and mute realizing life's eerily resemblance of her own less than two decades from when she had me. A mirror such as that can make you freeze.

Worse, resembling the man who'd betrayed her did not help one darn bit. After all, why would she help him or anything from him? He had lied to her. Destroyed her life. So, for me, it is what it is. She has always chosen the path of least resistance. It is an easier avenue to turn away, turn around, and not look in the rear view, than to confront what is happening in her face or with her knowledge, or both.

Sadly, the silence was its own kind of betrayal.

I didn't *just* feel abandoned by her—I felt erased. Forgotten. Like I was living through something I wasn't supposed to talk about, wasn't allowed to feel confused by or hurt by. I had to make sense of adult consequences with a child's understanding.

Years later, I would look back and ask myself hard questions about Teko, my mother, and about myself. I had to untangle the attention from the affection, the silence from the shame, the facts from the fiction. And I'd learn—slowly, painfully—that love doesn't demand your obedience, and protection doesn't always come in the form of rules. Sometimes it comes in a single, brave sentence: *"This isn't okay. You deserve better."* But I never heard that. So, I had to say it to myself, over and over until it stuck. I had to rely on my faith and believe it would get better, all while still trying to make my way in life.

These are some of the things that lingered in my mind through adulthood.

Moving on, leaving Teko in my rearview was supposed to be the end of the pain, at least that is how I reasoned. The pain of the poor choices, that ass whoopin' on Buckroe indeed was the end of that sad short time that lasted for what felt like forever vowing to myself to never be in THAT position AGAIN! But what I didn't realize at the time is when you walk away from someone or something who had so much control over you during such an early developmental time in your growth is the damage and destruction done to your self-worth at such a foundational level requires repair. Good thing I had good bones for it. Turns out I needed it.

I walked onto Hampton Institute (now Hampton University) college campus thinking I was free. I had no curfews, no watchful eyes, no elders influencing my every move. But what I realized is that I had missed essential developmental phases in socializing because of my relationship with Teko. He robbed me of those critical steps within that phase that would have taught me things about myself. I seemed to not know who I was without someone telling me. I didn't know how to be Fonda because I didn't really know who she was. All I know is that I was desperate to be seen, to be liked, and to be wanted. That same neediness he used against me didn't disappear—it just took on new forms.

While I have kept some of my same girlfriends close over the years, I found myself clinging to any male that would give me attention. These men, I'd hoped to find myself in. I was looking for the kind of love that had eluded me, or so I thought. Imagine, searching for such a love, at 17. It is crazy to think someone so young would find someone to spend a lifetime with. It is rare. But for me, each time I found myself in front of a mirror, I began to see my mother. That realization irritated me beyond words. I literally hated that I'd become her and I believed she felt the same without preventing any of it.

Socially awkward, there were times I was loud, wanting to be noticed, and other times I was quiet when I thought silence might earn affection, attention, or both. I'd laugh out loud when shit was not funny at all, staying up all night waiting for calls from the hall phone, and chasing relationships that mirrored the same imbalances I'd thought I'd left behind.

Meanwhile, I was failing, not just emotionally—academically too.

In the summer pre-college program and freshman year, I was an outstanding student. But the more I became socialized the more I began slipping. I told myself it was an adjustment at first. By second year midterms, I knew the truth: I was drowning. I skipped classes because I lost both focus and interest. I'd stare at the pages of textbooks, and nothing would stick. My mind was a fog, my heart was heavy as a shelf cloud, and I was exhausted from pretending everything was okay. There were days I found myself doing my new love interest Mayo's course work and not my own. "Type this just like it reads," he'd say. I asked, "okay, but you know that is plagiarism?" which he clearly didn't care anything about, and they were not quite checking for.

Mayo was part of the Divine Nine, an Omega Psi Phi. In Black culture there is nothing more satisfying than being in a Historically Black College or University. Being in the company of a Que was a highlight then. Oh, but if I only really knew back then. The frat house parties were legendary. The social life was lit. Those times seemed like blips on a screen and moments in time. His love for me, sex with me, and time spent with me were all transactional in my opinion. Mayo was seven years my senior. By then, he was considered an OG Que at Hampton. And for me, I was back on that sad ass merry-go-round. Same behavior, different day, different man. As things began to unravel for me, again, I didn't even stay at the dorm for the comfort of his ridiculously oversized bed in his space at the frat house. I had a vice. I never was good at drinking. I couldn't hold liquor, but I had my share of whiskey sours. Although youngin' was smoking weed, I wasn't because they were lacing it with formaldehyde, a.k.a. PCP, calling it 'love boat.' I was always so scared of that shit, so I stuck with my Virginia Slims, consigning to dying legally.

On the other side of the love boat, crack had begun to emerge, becoming the prevalent drug of choice but had not quite reared its ugly head in full in Southeastern Virginia. During this time in my life, I avoided all contact and connection from home, even though my granddaddy was footin' the bill. I didn't want to admit that I had gotten out of a toxic relationship, only to fall into another toxic cycle—with myself and with a body that was abused.

After that debacle of a relationship, I started to see a guy named Mike that I had been attracted to since high school. I really liked him. Having sex with him was different. He was caring, sensual, meaningful, and protective. The bonus was that I absolutely adored his family, all his brothers and sisters. It was like they had their own tribe. I loved how they loved on one another and showed up for one another. His family always showed me so much love and I felt right at home with his mom, Mrs. Suzy Q and his dad. His parents knew my grandparents and they both knew some of the same people from North Carolina.

As much as we enjoyed being with one another, it just wasn't in the cards for us. He accused me of something that I simply could not forgive. The kind of thing that will make you walk away without transportation. He created a wound with such huge weight that compounded the trauma I already experienced. All of this within a 24-month period post high school graduation.

After that, I felt invisible, exposed, and empty. It was clear I didn't know what I was doing when it came to affairs of the heart. I wasn't as "grown" as I thought I was. And just like my granddaddy told me, life was now teaching me better than he could tell me. It seemed like shame had put me in the place it wanted me to be once again and followed me everywhere.

That summer, I stood at a bus stop holding a manila folder with negative health results—no STDs, hallelujah, thank you Jesus—in one hand. On the other hand, a white envelope with debt notices from college. I asked myself, *Now what?*

By the end of my second semester of my second year, I was out of money, out of motivation, out of time and out of patience by my grandparents' account. Withdrawing from college was a disappointing and embarrassing moment for me and my family. I had no fight left in me. I just had a quiet understanding that whatever my dreams about college—all of it was slipping through my fingers.

I didn't have a car for transportation. I didn't have a job. I didn't have a backup plan. But I knew one thing with absolute clarity: I needed discipline. Not the punishment kind—but the structure kind. The kind that builds you back brick by brick. The kind that says get up, show up, don't quit. The kind that says people are watching to see if you're gonna stay down there or get up.

And that's what led me to the recruiter's office.

Joining the military was not a childhood dream or family tradition. Sure, my uncle had served in the Army and came back from Vietnam mentally damaged, without receiving a hero's welcome. For me, it was a lifeline, a necessity, a form of survival. I didn't walk into the recruiter's office with pride—I walked in with resolve. I needed structure. I needed food, shelter, a paycheck. I needed to stop emotionally hemorrhaging from years of self-sabotage and being mishandled and misunderstood. And if I'm being honest, I needed someone—something—to tell me who I was again. To teach me how to be strong without needing someone else to define me.

So, I signed the papers. Scared. Worn out. But determined. I didn't know it then, but I wasn't just enlisting in the military. I was enlisting in myself. I left on a Greyhound bus from the bus station literally right up the street from the house I grew up in. A Champs turned Greyhound Bus Station. I did my basic training and Advanced Individual Training (AIT) at Fort (Hell-Hole) Jackson, South Carolina.

Basic training and AIT stripped me down physically, mentally, spiritually. But in the place of all I had lost, there was a strange comfort in the uniformity, in being told exactly what to do, when to do it, and how to move forward. It made me feel, for a while, like I belonged to a group of people who were just like me. All of us searching for something.

But the silence I had carried into from high school to college came with me to basic—and it grew heavier. My silence was tested early.

I was assaulted in basic training. Not by a fellow trainee but by someone I knew. By a man who outranked me. A senior non-commissioned officer who knew just how the system worked—and how easy it was to exploit it. He knew that I had no one to tell, no power, and that if I dared say a word, I would be branded the problem. The liar. The one "out of line." I didn't say a word. I kept my mouth shut and my eyes forward. I needed my benefits. That was the unspoken rule. *Stay silent. Stay safe. Keep benefits.* I carried that rule with me into every drill weekend, every mobilization. It wrapped around me like my issued uniform—stiff, impersonal, and expected to fit no matter how it felt.

Then came Active Duty. Desert Shield. Desert Storm. The opportunity to serve for a full-time reservists and gain benefits that we normally only see if we are active. What should have been a moment of honor and purpose became another battlefield entirely—off the record. Behind the command post, the chain of command wasn't just about rank, it was about looking good to the next ranked officer and command.

There were whispers, always. Women warned each other with looks, not words. A quiet code of survival. Especially with mixed service. Don't be alone with him. Don't walk that corridor after lights out. Don't talk too much. Don't drink anything you didn't pour yourself. I wish I could say it only happened once. But it didn't. Every unit has them. There were more assaults. More hands that didn't ask permission. More power play, I left my body just to make it through the moment. I needed my 180 consecutive days. If I say something, I will go home. And the quest benefits start all over again as a reservist. And every time, I asked myself: *Who will believe me if I tell them? Who will protect me from the ones in charge?* The answers were always the same. No one. Because it wasn't just individual predators—it was the culture.

The senior NCOs and the commissioned officers worked hand in hand—not always directly, but in quiet conspiracy. Because no one wanted to do THAT kind of paperwork and have it on THEIR record. The silence demanded wasn't verbally enforced with threats. It was enforced with performance reports, lost promotions, changed orders, and invisible marks on your record that said *"troublemaker."* I watched good women get promoted over sorry ass men. Some women moved from unit to unit under the radar. Labels like "unfit" and "unstable" were bestowed on women who were smarter and wiser. While the men who broke them rose through the ranks with a chest full of medals and nothing but smoke in their wake, I stayed silent. I got my 180 consecutive days. Because in the military, silence is not just protection—it's survival.

But survival is not healing. I learned how to shoot a weapon, clean a barracks, and march in formation. But I never learned how to speak my truth out loud. I buried it. Each abuse of power. Every betrayal. In promotion ceremonies watching those who had hurt taken advantage of the system. I buried it under duty, under patriotism, under fear, under survival. And the silence—the one that started when I was a girl and trusted the wrong man—kept growing into a malignant silent tumor. Louder than any weapon I ever fired. Heavier than any pack I ever carried.

CHAPTER 11

Purpose in the Pain

With wisdom, I've gained the perspective that before the age of 10, I shouldn't have known what getting a feeling was. I should never have felt like I wasn't wanted, well-liked, or loved. I should've been genuinely cared for by the parents who brought me into this world and fiercely protected by every individual I encountered before I was old enough to do it properly. Most of all, I know I should've said something about all the ways I was feeling and the things going on then—the confusion, the sadness, the hurt, the anger, the hopelessness, the despair. Without giving thought to my feelings and words to those thoughts, I remained in a cage of silence that had only just begun to break. As I've said before, although many things in my life were shaped by what I went through in my childhood, I'm not willing to dwell on regret over any of it. Understanding my journey is the only path I am willing to take. I don't believe God allows things to happen for us to regret them. I believe He will enable them to happen and use them to bring us closer to Him. I believe God allows everything to happen for His reasons and in His seasons. He doesn't make mistakes nor wastes His time. His time is His, and His alone. I believe I'm here to testify as a sign of my faith that my words have helped heal the wrongs to right. Shedding light on the darkness of my past has been healing.

At the beginning of this story, I said that I received a wake-up call, which I also hesitated to answer. I let that phone ring, volume unchecked, for what I can only recall now to be an uncountable amount of time. Before I encountered the hashtag 'METOO,' I was healing. Decades earlier, I was finally done with

Teko and truly began to take the necessary steps to break free. Yet the trauma I endured as a young person had been so profound that it was difficult for me to recognize where the deep scars began and the superficial scar tissue ended.

When I was young, I rebelled against being misunderstood, often doing things that didn't align with my true self. Subconsciously, it was to show the absurdity of hidden truths. *How absurd is it to be beautiful, vulnerable, vibrant, and imaginative just to be unloved, unprotected, cast aside, and manifested into trauma and shame?* The result of this double-mindedness perpetuated a traumatic cycle of secrecy in my life. In terms of my support system, it became compartmentalized. I had the people I dealt with over here and the people I dealt with over there, and each received a different version of Fonda. It was all I thought I had to do to remain in people's good graces—to stay in their lives and keep them in mine. When life showed me how risky it was to let my complete, authentic self show, I stopped doing that. I often wondered without words how anyone could ever love and protect someone they didn't honestly know, all the while keeping some of the deepest parts of my being locked away out of fear. I was most afraid that the love and protection I so desperately desired might come at a steep price that I wasn't willing to pay. The chameleon-like skin I began to wear was a double-edged sword, one side of the blade to protect me from rejection and the other, leaving wounds cut from abandonment. I convinced myself that I had to be all these different people because I didn't want to be alone.

I had been programmed from a young age to believe that the greatest power I held was my ability to remain silent. If I didn't share my authentic experiences, then my grandfather would stay alive and out of jail, my mom would love and take me in, and no one would know of my boyfriend's abuse and he wouldn't leave me, among other things. These were the thoughts of a scared little girl hoping to stop bad things from happening to her all by staying silent. As a result, I bottled up many of my emotions and masked them whenever I suspected they might put me on the spot and cause problems for anybody involved. In the long run, the worst problem that showed up was my self-destructive behavior. I was constantly transforming into someone who I was not, simply to be liked by those who rarely cared about me. Now I know I'm not everybody's cup of tea, and that's okay. Nobody is.

I know I've always held strong opinions, and the more confidence I gain through wisdom, the more straightforward and cocky I can become, delivering those opinions no matter what space I'm occupying, at will. It's why I got temporarily canceled on Facebook for expressing my comments about Mr. Richard Stacy under a post announcing his death. On a different level, it's ultimately why my mother and I rarely speak now. Generally, we communicate via texts; sometimes she responds, and sometimes she does not. Either way, I understand. I can acknowledge that we hold feelings that make us not want to communicate. But I'm also willing to put those aside for the greater good of our relationship because time waits for no one. In this way, I've concluded the thought of never say never to God's possibilities.

For most of my life, I've felt this turmoil within myself and my relationship with my mother, the things that happened, and I finally understand. Now that I'm in my 60s, moving into a different season, I'm thinking about what's most important to me. The things I say that are not that important, I toss them to the side. There's no point in wasting breath and time. It's the things I do that are important. In my attempt to mend the relationship with my mother, I have had to extend her grace for being in an unimaginable situation when she was young. Only after going through what I did with Teko and working on myself did I realize that I was my mother's spitting image. I must also allow her to be however she wants as an aging human. I refuse to be mad at her in her 80s for doing whatever she wants. She's in her 80s. Everybody doesn't make it to see 80. She reserves the right to not ever do anything she doesn't want to do, as well as do whatever she wants. If the Lord lets me see that age, I will be the same way.

Imagine the 30,000-foot view of being raised by an older man, my grandfather. The unintended consequences of full disclosure are an attraction to older men and being married twice to older men. In my second marriage, my husband is 18 years my senior. Imagine how broken and conflicted I was when I showed up in this union. I know my husband loves me unconditionally, and I love him. We fiercely protect one another. He is the best thing that has ever happened to and for me and my children. We built this beautiful life together with a beautiful blended family. Nevertheless, what I experienced early in life resulted in those choices. Understanding myself and navigating my emotions has been a journey through mental health. To explain it better, not only was I raised by an older man but victimized by another and spent the better part of my life being unconditionally loved by another. It was such a prevalent occurrence and recurrence in my life that it feels surreal. It was difficult for me to understand at that age that it wasn't my fault. After all, I felt like I chose to be in some situations, and others, I was put in. Nevertheless, there came a particular time when it was apparent that I'd grown up too quickly, and what I understood to be true about myself and the world was immature and underdeveloped, at best. My remedy then became my willingness to view my life in a different light—to reimagine it as one filled with grace, favor, forgiveness, joy, and peace.

For a very long time, my thoughts and feelings were hijacked, held hostage by realizations of abandonment and abuse to the point where, at times, it felt like they were controlling me, either forced to fight, flee, or freeze due to strong emotions rooted in fear. Looking back, my slow start to let go of the things that harmed me in the past is attributed to my lack of acknowledgment that I could change things for the better. Motherhood played a significant role in how I was able to heal from my childhood wounds. For one, it made me understand that my mother wasn't the cold, unfeeling monster I created her to be. She's human, just like me. And whatever decisions she might've made in the past concerning me were restricted; she only did the best she could do for her life at the time.

When Dessa left me after I was born, I concluded that it wasn't just about her. The decision wasn't as simple as leaving her little chocolate baby or obeying her father's rules to leave me. No. Motherhood is tough work. Depending on the year or the decade and your place in the world, the circumstances you're up against, and the cultural implications of it all, you're going to make mistakes as a mom no matter what your decisions are. Sometimes those mistakes hurt you and your child in ways that you never could've imagined. Becoming a mother myself helped me empathize with the woman who gave birth to me. Going through my journey of motherhood allowed me to sympathize with my mother's sacrifice she made for me to have a better life. Her reasons were all for the best. My mother has shared with me on several occasions, to my surprise, how she wishes she could've done for me what I did for my kids. My response to her was always, "It's okay. We can start from here." Our problem was failure to launch.

At any given moment, I will readily admit that I'm not perfect, which might explain why you might've cringed at some of the things I've shared so far or how I've decided to share them. As a perfect example, if you talk to anybody who knows me and my family when it comes to my daughters, they'll always say, "Your girls are the best." That is true. They are indeed the best, despite me. You don't know what they went through with me. As a bug on the wall in one therapy session would be all I needed to know, my girls experienced pain with me. They'd probably say I was a terror! I can only say that I did the best I could. I raised them with the familiarity of my grandaddy and grandmamma through love and protection, first and foremost. Did I do or get everything right? No, I did not. I fucked up. A lot.

There would be times when I did not communicate with them in the most tender of ways. I cursed at them. I called them out of their names. Shit that I would beat someone on the streets for doing. There is no excusing that. I can only admit I was a young, inexperienced mother who went through some shit that left me without the tools to be a mother in a tender-hearted way.

Nonetheless, I showed up. I made it a point to attend all their sports games and school events. Showing up to me was the very definition of being a present parent. I watched them like a hawk. Because I was so determined to be present in their lives, I couldn't hide my flaws. I had to learn that presence brings imperfection. When you stay away long enough, nobody gets to see how you fail, how you get back up, or who you truly are, so they have a tendency to see you as perfect, without any faults. I couldn't get away with that perfection thing because I was too busy being authentically present, and sometimes that presence brought embarrassment for them. Like the time I got put out of the gym during one of my daughter's traveling basketball games because I was 'cussing' the refs out over bad calls. I'm not saying that any of this justifies my behavior when I yelled at them loud or expected too much. I can guarantee two things: One, their lists of grievances on how they grew up does not include me ever allowing a grown man to violate them while they were still vulnerable little girls. Two, it's because of this fierce commitment of mine to love and protect them that I eventually saw the error of my ways and grew the capacity to love differently to take the appropriate steps toward greater change. And I still mess up from time to time, but I won't stop, can't stop trying! I ain't my mother.

Before this point, I couldn't fathom what life could've been like for Dessa as she was raising me. Her focus on the past and what didn't go right in her own life left it nearly impossible for her to give us the chance we both needed to thrive. Before today, I was similar to my mother in her focus on the past. Because of what I'd been through, I spent many days believing I was unworthy of love. This belief led to low self-esteem, depression, anxiety in the form of eczema, uncontrollable anger, countless fights, infidelity in my first marriage, and, above all else, another instance of sexual assault in the military in my adulthood. Truth is, I am still a work in progress, but remain focused on the present and do not allow the pain of my past to get to me. It was indeed an uphill battle to get here, and trust me, I backslide sometimes, but it is progress, not perfection. There have been many times when I've found myself taking one baby step forward and two gigantic elephant steps back. Abandonment recovery can be tricky like that. Today, I can see how the losses I experienced throughout my childhood are what made me grow into the individual I am now.

Whether it was through the loss of my biological parents when they both left me, or the loss of my innocence at the hands of child predators, I grew the most each time I decided to push forward in life despite how those losses made me feel. Learning to love life and others through those experiences molded me into the fierce protector I'm known to be. No children under my protection and entrusted to me ever had to worry about being preyed upon because I was a fierce protector. I know the signs, and I paid the price. It just won't happen on my watch. I'll go to jail or die first. For me, it was a blessing, and it was my duty to protect kids who came under my roof and my umbrella of limitless protection. It was my call to do just what I am doing. Go through the fire, live to testify, love, and protect.

The fact that I was able to raise, care for, and feed multiple children who came through our home is something I've always taken pride in. It doesn't matter to me whether you're an uncle or a momma, an older cousin or a close "friend," I'm watching everything and everybody. So, people can call me what they want to, but what they won't do is call me complacent or complicit in the harming of a child.

For the majority of my life, my pain-plagued trauma found me struggling to think coherently and make sense of the lies that I'd grown to believe about myself. I had to figure out how to cope in order to get work done. I learned to be a better listener, which helped me communicate more effectively with my coworkers. I started reading a lot to learn more about myself and the world around me, then committed myself to practicing the words that stood out from every page. When I failed at things, sometimes miserably, I found ways to pick myself back up and try again without beating myself down or allowing anyone else to do the same. I ate a little better and pushed my body out of its discomfort, even if that movement meant just a short walk outside, no matter the weather. To get to this place of peace, I had to feel the rain, the sun, and the wind on my skin to ground myself and know that I was alive, and that my life had a purpose. Sometimes, I'd return inside from my walks and immediately lay down for a nap because I was so tired. Listening to my body when it told me it needed rest was a life-changing experience. Soon after, I stopped making excuses for myself and others when I wasn't being taken care of, and I began to stand in that space for all of us, ready to hold myself accountable for what I could and could not do to love me.

A few things have helped, but not without a sustained applied effort on my part. Reading the works of bell hooks, "Sister of the Yam," and Susan Anderson, "The Journey from Abandonment to Healing," as they discuss the acts of love in healing abandonment, has allowed me to make considerable strides toward healing. Listening to various audiobooks, and podcasts, and watching Iyanla Vanzant's programming online and on TV, like "Iyanla Fix My Life," can sometimes energize me a bit more as an alternative to reading books about addressing my problems. You know the saying "you think you got problems until you hear about somebody else's." Then you thank God for the blessed life you lead. My mindfulness journey and practice, as well as yoga, relaxes me.

Each author and app has given me the tools and inspiration to elevate to a notable level beyond my issues.

To reconnect with my healthy body—the one that existed before being torn apart at the seams, inside and out, I've had to get creative about leaning into uncomfortability. Not too long ago, I was in a series of Mind-Body therapies with the VA, or the United States Department of Veterans Affairs. For those who are unfamiliar, the VA helps military vets with all things from healthcare to cemetery services. This time around they were helping me strengthen my mental health during a two-hour block from 1 p.m. to 3 p.m. that met every Tuesday for 10 weeks—some of these sessions I had to fight my way through. Confronting the scars of loneliness, abuse, and degradation was difficult to do out loud in a group session. Acknowledging the feelings that followed this work almost felt more painful than living through their initial onset. That's the bittersweet deal with out-of-body experiences that save us from the brunt of our traumas. At the moment, we don't have to feel all the pain of what's happening until the precise time when it begins to confront you to clear those feelings from the past, that the aged pain is recognizably refined and amplified. Only God knows why this is. I know there were times that I didn't want to go through the process. I didn't want to deal with the feelings that I spent most of my life running away from. Towards the end of my scheduled weeks, I started to feel like I wanted to do anything other than feel better, but I'm grateful that I could say, "No, you're going to continue to show up for yourself. And even if you're not getting anything out of the day, something worthwhile will be revealed to you." Each time I did that, I was glad that I did. Completing the entirety of that series made me mindful of soft belly breathing, the art, or lack thereof, that happens when you doodle and draw to visualize *this is where I am, this is where I want to be,* and all the little things that help me to be well, like just taking some time out of my day to find a place and a space to breathe and take in nature as it is, to make sure that my feet are grounded. I like walking barefoot in the grass. It reminds me of home. Just doing these things helps calm me when my mind is chaotic. It's indeed been a long time coming.

The 1991 Daily Press article I previously mentioned states that Teko "waited until he had no more reservations about working his recovery program so he could feel good about himself first…" For me, I waited until I could bear no more pain to write this book and tell my account of what happened to me, and the #METOO movement gave me the strength to do it. I agree. There are several reasons he'd prefer to forget much of the 80s. One of the main reasons is because he was a predator and a pedophile during the 80s when he groomed young girls in the Newport News Public School System. He was supposed to be a coach to this kid he used to mark me. This young Black boy was as much a victim by helping him as I was.

Along with these misgivings, I'm sure he would prefer to forget many other things, too. Looking back, it was only God's grace covering me that brought me here, and that's not something I ever want to forge or take for granted. I respect my journey and honor it by bravely sharing my story with those who will listen.

Everything I went through, I went through for reasons I may never fully come to know or understand. But I'm certain this book is one of those reasons I am intimately aware of. I've come all this way to tell you a story you need to hear. Now is the time to notice that if you were born into this world, you have a purpose. The beautiful thing is that God has divinely appointed this purpose to you, and you only. Each of us has our talents. What is God's divine purpose for you? What is your talent? Everybody's journey is their journey, and we each must run our race. I've learned that when you're on a similar path to someone else, getting to know their story makes a significant difference in your ability to protect yourself against the mistakes made. If your desire is to be loved by someone who was supposed to love you, and you are abused—it could be a mother, father, sibling, family member, even a close friend, or romantic love interest—please know that abuse in any form, is not love. More importantly, know that anyone who sees something happening to you, around you or actively participates and doesn't say a word about the abuse is complicit, and they are part of the problem. For years, I caused an immense amount of harm and pain to myself and others because I was silent about all the things that kept hurting me. But God. He brought me out of that cycle of trauma and bad habits. Nobody else would or could, not even myself. That's all I can say when I look back on my life. He has constantly been there for me. You need to verbalize this out loud to somebody, if but no one else, yourself in the mirror. I had to believe something greater than myself could save me. People fall short all the time. My faith in God strengthened me when it felt like all I wanted to do was give up on becoming better.

It doesn't mean my faith has absolved every harm against me, nor has it righted their wrongs against me. I have managed to give people the benefit of the doubt. I extended a notable level of undeserved grace. I've forgiven a lot of people, for me. Not for them. Growth, for me, is fighting the urge to accept the things I cannot change and let the karmic energy of the universe happen for good.

When I was a child, I thought as a child. I disrespected my mother, my grandparents, and my family. I am so sorry and I apologized. The times I stayed in situations, knowing I was wrong, I forgave and apologized to myself. I disrespected myself, and the sanctity of a young married couple who was going through rough times, and I apologized. I never want to miss an opportunity to acknowledge what is wrong and try to make it right. Those apologies weren't always welcomed or outright received, but they were given unconditionally, not based on acceptance. The apologies were for me. Learning to forgive yourself is instrumental in mental health recovery. Particularly for those who experience sexual grooming, sexual assault, and abandonment.

My ability to let go and let God was easier. I realized God had so much more in store for me than what I was trying to hold on to. When we purge from something, it is a painful process. The willingness to hold on is so strong it becomes a forced release. What you come to understand about the effects of purging is how it frees you from the one thing causing so much discomfort and pain down in your gut. When reality sets after experiencing the vile nature of throwing up and out, you feel better. You can fully digest again. The same is true with my physical tension in my body. My fists were so tight and clinched, holding on to the pain of what happened to me, that my hand could not fully receive and realize God's blessings. "A closed fist can't catch water," as my granddaddy would say.

I didn't realize until after I entered therapy that I was able to connect with my inner child and realize how much pain I was dealing with. Some of those thoughts continue to live within me today, but don't haunt me. It is for her, not me, that letting go is much easier said than done. But I continue to try for her. I show up for myself. I hear my granddaddy's voice saying, "Stop thinking about the things you want to do and just do. You do nothing; you come to nothing." In many ways, this book is my direct response to that call to action to free my inner child, the little girl in me, from the hidden pain and horrific consequences of her silence, to rid her of her inability to recognize that she is loved. I believe this work begins and ends with a mirror—this time, I see clearly.

To all the young ladies who were strong enough to stand up and speak your truth about once being innocent prey to a sexual predator, I see you. If you've yet to share these experiences with anyone, I pray you gain strength through my story, as I've gained strength from the inspiration of our shared resilience. No matter what your story is, you don't have to play the part of the victim forever. As the main character, you can decide that there is no more room left on your stage for victims to exist. You can succeed beyond that status and enjoy the fruits of your labor, knowing that you were courageous enough to make a necessary change and protect yourself, and the others around you. And that time for success may not be here yet. Like my life, it could take decades before you get to a place where you feel comfortable enough to go through the discomfort of acknowledging the wrongs you had nothing to do with but endured, whether you can make them right or not. Just know that it doesn't matter how old you are now or how old you were when it happened, whatever *it* was. The moment you decide to take ownership of your story and share it openly and honestly with others, even if it's just one person for one minute, that's when you'll begin to free yourself from the greatest pain known to humankind: the pain of being yourself.

During my senior year of high school, I was silently suffering from some of the worst pain imaginable. This was the time I discovered who my true friends were. I asked my girlfriends for their opinion on whether my life was going well or not. I'd found the security within our relationship to tell them things that were nearly impossible for me to voice to any other group of people. My BFFs Deborah and Ra have been my confidants and friends for over five decades. They knew how molestation and grooming affected me. Deborah was always the friend that said, "It's about you. It's your story to tell. I won't tell you what to do. And don't let anybody else tell 'ya either! Whatever you need me to do, I'm here." Deborah is the one who will be sitting in jail next to me because we decided to fight the world over each other's battles. If you ever heard of a "ride or die," she's that chick. Deborah is in charge of quality management and has the details. Ra, she's that strategic cut card. She has outside-the-box solutions. I'd hold 'em. She hit 'em. She has the succession plan and is helping me navigate my time, my way. She's the planner, always thinking ahead and the keeper of secrets. I owe my life to these ladies in ways I cannot explain. If you are lucky to have one, you are blessed.

People always talk about how it takes a village to raise a child, but I think about the things that happened in my childhood, and I want to rework the phrase to say that it takes a village to raise a *community* where children can grow. I see a village of people as a group of those who are hyperaware—they can spot threats from a mile away and have a way of knowing when something will benefit everybody, not just a few. These villages can create thriving communities where the children can grow up without abuse because the people watching over every last bit of their lives are vigilant. I've learned that every family has an Uncle Nasty and an Auntie Feely, but the people of the village know this, and we ensure that somebody's always watching them, whether inside or outside the house. Watch the village.

My village helped me pick up the pieces and my friends' mothers, Ms. Roberta, Ra's Mom, Ms. Leona, Deborah's Mom, and Ms. Helen, G's mom. My friends sharing their moms with me wasn't the bonus. It was the families that came along with them that made all the difference. God used these surrogate moms to demonstrate His unwavering love for me.

Every child needs protection. Every young person on this planet deserves to be watched over, looked after, and cared for—to live without expecting that information to blow up in my face. Be aware. Use your voice. Protect children and always hold their predators accountable, regardless of what that looks like or means. Find support, whether it's individual or group, because it's crucial. Always be bold enough to say something when you see harm inflicted ANYWHERE, and even if it scares you, stand in that gap. No matter what happens, God's grace gives us a chance to always try again. Lastly, to the young Black girl who is always willing to do the hard things that bring peace and liberation, you are seen, appreciated, and encouraged. I hope you enjoy the happy life you deserve.

ACKNOWLEDGMENTS

To my husband, Charles J. Woodard, my soulmate, the love of my life, and my rock! We define real Black love through trust and forgiveness. You have demonstrated how unconditional commitment transforms everlasting love. To my children, Fevia & Derek, Ferin & Gregory, thank you for your love and support. It is the absolute honor of my life to be your mother. Fevia and Ferin, I am so proud of the women and mothers you have become. I cherish how you love your children, my 'grands,' when I witness how you tenderly mother. Derek and Gregory, you are such quality young Black men and excellent fathers. I am so proud of the dedicated girl dad and dedicated boy dad you are. As couples, your young, beautiful Black love is a beacon of hope to all who bear witness. Keep striving for #BlackLoveGoals in your respective ways, and always keep God first and foremost in everything you do. To my bonus children, Charles Lamont and Charlette, I sincerely have been honored to be your bonus mom. Our relationship has become one of the most beautiful blended families anyone could ever ask for.

A special acknowledgement to my ten grandchildren, Gregory II, Victoria, Giovani, twins Ava, and Nadia, Giannis, and my angel granddaughter in heaven, super Nova E, who watches over all of us. You are the very best part of me. You are my gifts from God. To my bonus grandchildren, Katelyn, Zoe, and Mason, it is a privilege of my life to be in and influence your life and to watch you grow. It is my prayer that each of your lives will be emotionally fuller, mentally healthier, and rewardingly more prosperous all because GG made a conscious effort to speak truth to power, forgive, heal—to be better and do better—all because when I'm better for myself, I'm better for you! Remember, when life challenges you, and it will, look in the mirror, adjust your crowns, and know who you are: Black "Kings" and "Queens" of a

Royal Tribe of Black | Native | Haitian People. Realize you are children of God. Know that you are my legacy, and each of you will change the world for the better.

To my grandparents watching over me, who showed me mercy and grace, Odell and Maggie Richardson, affectionately known as Daddy and Momma, thank you for feeding me, clothing me, and threading hard work into the fabric of my life. Thank you for telling me that an example is just an example, not to make more of it than it is, and to know there is no such thing as a good or a bad example. Instead, it is an example of what to do or what not to do. It is solely an "example" all by itself, for it's "the mainest thang."

To my mother, thank you for giving me life! Your example changed the trajectory of my life. You've inspired me to cultivate change and mind the gap in my life and the lives I am responsible for. Brené Brown coined the phrase in her book, "Daring Greatly," the concept of minding the gap as "being the space between where we're standing and where we want to be." I found the courage to mind the gap between being present and available as I closed the disengagement divide between mother and daughter, navigating through life the best way I know how. Your absence and inaudible motivation redefined and shaped me to be something constructive and beautiful in this world.

My life is mine. I have a renewed sense of purpose and meaning because I finally found the courage to speak truth to power. My silence has broken like a high-grade fever. My words no longer shut up in my bones. I am no longer in emotional exile—thank God! I do not see a victim in the mirror anymore. I know I am a survivor. I am motivated by the desire to be whole and free. I woke up a different kind of woman with a different type of strength and renewed hope. My strength comes from God. What I went through was intentional to bring forth the testimony of His power. I am no longer weak. I am no longer silent. It is an understatement to say I know and believe in my heart God's grace and mercy are sufficient.

From the womb, God has covered my life. He ordained it for His purpose, covered by His hands. I am so grateful.

Last but certainly not least, I want to thank activists Tarana Burke and Common for encouraging hope in this world to people like me because "#METOO" will "let LOVE have the last word." You will never know how your advocacy and sharing your testimony in your books helped me on my healing journey. Susan Anderson, words cannot explain how your book, "The Journey from Abandonment to Healing," was paramount to my recovery. I am grateful for the reminder that "commitment to love" is the antidote to abandonment. Karen C.L. Anderson, your emails, shared experiences, and book "Difficult Mothers, Adult Daughters" let me know I was in good company. It was significant in helping me manage and understand me and my mother's relationship. It's not just me, after all. Brené Brown, thank you for reminding me, "I AM ENOUGH!" RAINN (Rape, Abuse & Incest National Network), your organization, is the singular source that took my call on your hotline on more than one occasion when I was at my lowest. The confidentiality and compassion volunteers showed gained my trust and helped me turn the corner from victim to survivor. I am eternally grateful. And thank you to the countless licensed clinical mental health professionals who do yeoman's work in individual and group therapy sessions! You all saved my life! I showed up for me!

ABOUT THE AUTHOR

FONDA E. WOODARD

ADVOCATE/AUTHOR/PUBLISHER

I'm an advocate and veteran. I served as a transportation specialist, career advisor, first sergeant, and retired civil servant for 36 years in the Federal Aviation Administration. I am the wife, mother of four, and a proud grandmother of 10, with one of them being an angel grandbaby. I have a Bachelor of Science in Management Studies and a minor in Women's Studies from the University of Maryland Global Campus. I am a native Virginian. I have dedicated my career to leadership, mentorship, and advocacy.

Now, making my author debut, I am using my voice to shed light on difficult but necessary conversations. "Never Said a Word" is my debut book. I offer my personal stories of abandonment, sexual grooming, and molestation. After feeling my voice had been silenced for far too long, I'm sharing my story raw and unfiltered.

Beyond writing, I am also the creator of aFEW Mindful Moments, a podcast that fosters meaningful discussions about healing, resilience, and personal growth. My blog, aFEW Lost Words, is where I share deeper reflections on the themes explored in my book. I will continue advocating for awareness, ensuring that the experiences of survivors, service members, veterans, and their families are heard and acknowledged.